BETTY CROCKER'S
SALADS

Golden Press • New York
Western Publishing Company, Inc.
Racine, Wisconsin

Photography Director: Len Weiss
Illustrator: Helen Federico

Third Printing, 1978

Printed in the U.S.A. by Western Publishing Company, Inc.
Published by Golden Press, New York, New York.
Library of Congress Catalog Card Number: 76-56961

Golden® and Golden Press® are trademarks of
Western Publishing Company, Inc.

CONTENTS

TOSSED GREEN SALADS

A collection with character — featuring Great Caesar Salad, Flaming Spinach Salad and many more. With combos like these, you'll find there's no such thing as a "plain" green salad.

5

FRUIT SALADS

Fresh, canned or frozen — fruits from all over the world star in top-billed salads for every season of the year. Serve as a first course, on the side or even as dessert.

21

VEGETABLE SALADS

For family fare or company occasions, vegetables take on a new look and a new importance. In salads — artfully arranged, gracefully molded or gently tossed. Take your choice.

41

MAIN-DISH SALADS

Menu-making made easy! Start with Marinated Beef and Mushrooms, Oriental Chicken Salad or any of these full-size salads. Just add a bread and a beverage to round out the meal.

53

Index
71

Dear Friend–

When you stop to think about it, salads just may be one of America's biggest contributions to the world's fare. Over the years we've reached into our gardens, cupboards and freezers to create an almost infinite variety of salads.

With their color, zest and contrast, salads are welcome anytime, anywhere– at buffet suppers, casual picnics, elegant luncheons, family meals. Particularly good choices for a party buffet are Cucumber Salad Mold or Chef's Smorgasbord Salad; picnics become *picniques* with Picnic Tomatoes or Lentil-Ham Salad; luncheon guests will dote on Crab-Shrimp-Avocado Salad or Tuna-Cantaloupe Salads.

Regular mealtime salads should be just as interesting as those served on special occasions. Why not enjoy different ones at different times? You can serve a salad at the start of the meal, with the meal, at the end of the meal, even as the meal.

An appetizer salad should be just that. Its intent is to stimulate the appetite, not satisfy it. As such, choose a salad that's light, with a delicate dressing. Tossed green or simple fruit or vegetable salads are first-course favorites.

A "go-along" salad should complement the main course as well as provide a contrast in color, texture and flavor–such as Eggplant Salad with roast lamb, Watercress and Asparagus Toss with chicken or Spinach and Sprouts Salad with baked ham.

An end-of-meal salad is usually on the sweet side, refreshing the taste buds and replacing the dessert course. Strawberry Freeze, 24-Hour Salad or any molded fruit salad will fill the bill.

Main-dish salads are, of course, heartier. They usually include meat, fish, poultry, cheese or eggs–singly or in combination.

On the following pages you'll find all of the salads mentioned here, as well as many other inviting, intriguing ideas and recipes. Included throughout, too, are coordinated dressings and helpful information–adding up to a complete guide for salads from start to serve.

Betty Crocker

TOSSED GREEN SALADS

Spectacular Ways to Bring on the Smiles

Turn over a new leaf with these crisp, light, health-full salads. When you're fixing and mixing greens, what goes together, when, if and how are all-important. So our directions are precise and our dressings are just right. But allowing for personal preferences, we've also included a wide-ranging make-your-own-salad chart. You'll find that these salads, particularly, seem to bloom with the little extra touch only you can toss in.

TOSSED SALAD CRISSCROSS

(for 6 to 8 servings)

Find your own favorites, then mix and match to suit the occasion.

Basic Salad Greens

Choose 1 or more to total 12 cups.

Iceberg lettuce Boston lettuce Bibb lettuce	Leaf lettuce Red leaf lettuce Romaine	Escarole Spinach Watercress	Endive (French or Belgian) Curly endive

Add Salad Sparkers

Choose 1 or more to total 1½ cups.

Fresh vegetables:	Radishes, sliced Tomato wedges Zucchini, sliced	Fruit:	Meat, fish and poultry:

Carrots, thinly
  sliced
Cauliflowerets
Celery, sliced or
  chopped
Cucumbers, sliced
  or cubed
Green peppers,
  chopped or sliced
Mushrooms, sliced
Onions, sliced or
  chopped
	Cooked vegetables:
	
	Artichoke hearts or
	  bottoms, plain or
	  marinated
	Dilled green beans
	Green peas, beans
	  or sliced carrots,
	  marinated
		Apples, cut into
		  wedges or sliced
		Avocados, sliced
		Orange sections
		Cheese:
		
		Parmesan, grated
		Swiss or Cheddar,
		  cut into strips
		  or cubes
			Ham, tongue or
			  cold cuts, cut into
			  strips or cubes
			Shrimp, crabmeat
			  or lobster, cut up
			Turkey or chicken,
			  cut up

Toss with . . .

Shake to mix.

¼ cup vegetable oil,
  olive oil or
  combination
	2 tablespoons cider,
	  wine or tarragon
	  vinegar
		¾ teaspoon salt
		⅛ to ¼ teaspoon
		  pepper
			1 small clove
			  garlic, crushed

Garnish with . . .

Choose 1 or 2.

Bacon, crisply fried,
  crumbled
Blue cheese,
  crumbled
	Carrot curls
	Cherry tomatoes
	Cocktail onions
		Croutons
		French fried onions
		Gherkins, sliced
			Hard-cooked eggs,
			  sliced
			Olives, sliced
			Salted nuts

GREAT CAESAR SALAD

Garlic Croutons (below)
Coddled Egg (below)
1 clove garlic, cut into halves
8 anchovy fillets, cut up
⅓ cup olive oil
1 teaspoon Worcestershire sauce
½ teaspoon salt
¼ teaspoon dry mustard
Freshly ground pepper
1 large or 2 small bunches romaine, torn into bite-size pieces
1 lemon
⅓ cup grated Parmesan cheese

Prepare Garlic Croutons and Coddled Egg. Rub large wooden salad bowl with cut clove of garlic. Allow a few small pieces of garlic to remain in bowl if desired. Mix anchovies, oil, Worcestershire sauce, salt, mustard and pepper in bowl; toss with romaine until leaves glisten. Break egg onto salad. Squeeze lemon over salad; toss. Sprinkle croutons and cheese over salad; toss.

6 servings.

Garlic Croutons
Heat oven to 400°. Trim crusts from 4 slices white bread. Butter both sides of bread slices generously; sprinkle slices with ¼ teaspoon garlic powder. Cut into ½-inch cubes. Bake in ungreased baking pan, 13x9x2 inches, stirring occasionally, until golden brown and crisp, 10 to 15 minutes.

Coddled Egg
Place cold egg in warm water. Heat enough water to boiling to cover egg completely. Immerse egg in boiling water with spoon; remove from heat. Cover and let stand 30 seconds. Immediately cool egg in cold water to prevent further cooking.

CREAMY LETTUCE TOSS

Sour Cream Dressing (below)
12 slices bacon
1 medium head iceberg lettuce, torn into bite-size pieces
3 green onions (with tops), finely chopped

Prepare Sour Cream Dressing. Fry bacon until crisp; drain, reserving 2 tablespoons bacon fat. Crumble bacon. Toss lettuce, onions, bacon and reserved bacon fat; toss with dressing.

6 servings.

Sour Cream Dressing
½ cup dairy sour cream or unflavored yogurt
1 tablespoon sugar
1 tablespoon vinegar
½ teaspoon salt

Mix all ingredients. *½ cup dressing.*

SALADE PROVENÇALE

2 large heads iceberg lettuce, torn into bite-size pieces
8 ounces spinach, torn into bite-size pieces
2 jars (about 7 ounces each) marinated artichoke hearts
2 cans (3⅞ ounces each) pitted ripe olives, drained
1 bottle (8 ounces) herb salad dressing

Divide lettuce and spinach between 2 large plastic bags; refrigerate. Just before serving, add 1 jar artichoke hearts (with liquid), 1 can olives and half of the salad dressing to each bag. Close bags tightly; shake vigorously. Serve in large bowl.

12 servings.

GOURMET TOSSED GREEN SALAD

1 medium head iceberg lettuce, torn
  into bite-size pieces
4 ounces mushrooms, sliced
1 small cauliflower, separated into
  tiny flowerets
1 small Bermuda onion, thinly sliced
  and separated into rings
1 medium green pepper, chopped
½ cup sliced pimiento-stuffed olives
½ cup crumbled blue cheese
  Classic French Dressing (below)

Toss lettuce, mushrooms, cauliflowerets, onion, green pepper, olives and cheese. Cover and refrigerate at least 1 hour. Just before serving, toss with Classic French Dressing.

8 to 10 servings.

Classic French Dressing
¼ cup olive oil, vegetable oil or
  combination
2 tablespoons wine or tarragon
  vinegar
¾ teaspoon salt
¼ teaspoon freshly ground pepper
¼ teaspoon monosodium glutamate
1 small clove garlic, finely chopped
  or crushed

Toss salad with oil until leaves glisten. Mix remaining ingredients; toss with salad.

FANTASTIC GREEN SALAD
Pictured on page 17.

9 cups bite-size pieces mixed salad
  greens (romaine, red leaf lettuce,
  leaf lettuce)
1 cup crumbled Gorgonzola cheese
  (about 4 ounces)°
  Generous dash of pepper
¼ cup vegetable oil
¼ cup tarragon vinegar

Place salad greens and cheese in bowl; sprinkle with pepper. Toss salad with oil until leaves glisten. Pour vinegar on salad; toss.

8 servings.

° Your favorite crumbly cheese (such as blue or feta) can be substituted for the Gorgonzola cheese. Or use 1 cup diced Gruyère or sharp Cheddar cheese.

MIXED GREENS WITH GARLIC DRESSING

Garlic Dressing (below)
8 cups bite-size pieces mixed salad
   greens (lettuce, curly endive, spinach)
1 cup cheese-and-garlic croutons

Prepare Garlic Dressing; toss with salad greens. Sprinkle with croutons.

4 servings.

Garlic Dressing
2 tablespoons vegetable oil
1 tablespoon plus 1½ teaspoons
   vinegar
1 teaspoon salt
¼ teaspoon prepared mustard
¼ teaspoon Worcestershire sauce
1 small clove garlic, crushed
   Dash of pepper

Shake all ingredients in tightly covered jar.
About ¼ cup dressing.

FLAMING SPINACH SALAD
Pictured on page 18.

12 ounces spinach, torn into bite-size
    pieces
¼ cup sliced celery
2 tablespoons sliced green onions
4 slices bacon, cut into ½-inch pieces
2 tablespoons packed brown sugar
2 tablespoons vinegar
¼ teaspoon salt
⅛ teaspoon dried tarragon leaves
    Dash of pepper
2 tablespoons brandy

Place spinach, celery and onions in serving dish. Fry bacon until crisp; drain on paper towels and reserve. Remove all but 1 tablespoon bacon fat from skillet. Stir brown sugar, vinegar, salt, tarragon and pepper into fat in skillet. Heat just to boiling; stir in bacon. Heat until bacon is hot; pour on spinach, celery and onions. Heat brandy just until warm; ignite and pour on salad. Toss and serve immediately.

4 servings.

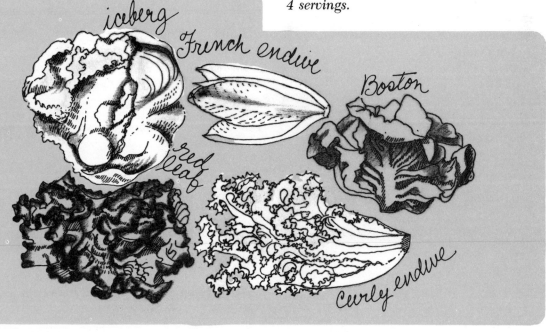

iceberg

French endive

Boston

red leaf

curly endive

GREENS AND TOMATO-TOMATO

Pumpernickel Croutons (below)
Tomato Dressing (below)
10 cups bite-size pieces mixed salad greens (iceberg lettuce, curly endive)
2 tomatoes, chopped

Prepare Pumpernickel Croutons and Tomato Dressing. Toss salad greens, tomatoes and dressing; sprinkle with croutons.

8 servings.

Pumpernickel Croutons
Heat oven to 400°. Trim crusts from 4 slices pumpernickel or dark rye bread. Brush both sides of bread slices generously with vegetable oil or butter or margarine, softened; sprinkle slices with salt and 1 teaspoon dried dill weed or about 1 tablespoon snipped fresh dill weed. Cut into ½-inch cubes. Bake in ungreased baking pan, 13x 9x2 inches, stirring occasionally, until golden brown and crisp, 10 to 15 minutes.

Tomato Dressing
½ can (10¾-ounce size) condensed tomato soup (about ½ cup)
⅓ cup vegetable oil
¼ cup packed brown sugar
¼ cup vinegar
1 tablespoon snipped chives
1 teaspoon onion salt
1 teaspoon paprika
½ teaspoon dry mustard

Mix all ingredients. *About 1¼ cups dressing.*

TOSSED GODDESS BEAN SPROUTS

Green Goddess Dressing (below)
8 cups bite-size pieces Bibb lettuce
1 can (16 ounces) bean sprouts, rinsed and drained

Prepare Green Goddess Dressing; toss with lettuce and bean sprouts.

8 servings.

Green Goddess Dressing
¾ cup mayonnaise or salad dressing
2 tablespoons finely snipped parsley
1 tablespoon finely chopped onion
2 or 3 anchovy fillets, finely chopped, or 2 to 3 teaspoons anchovy paste
2 teaspoons tarragon wine vinegar
1 clove garlic, crushed

Mix all ingredients. *About 1 cup dressing.*

WATERCRESS AND ASPARAGUS TOSS
Pictured on page 17.

Lime Dressing (below)
3 bunches watercress, torn into bite-size pieces
1 pound asparagus, cut diagonally into thin slices

Prepare Lime Dressing; toss with watercress and asparagus.

6 servings.

Lime Dressing
¼ cup vegetable oil
Juice of 1 lime (about 1 tablespoon plus 1½ teaspoons)
½ teaspoon salt

Shake all ingredients in tightly covered jar. *About ⅓ cup dressing.*

KNOW YOUR SALAD GREENS

*There's a wide world of greens out there. Get to know them—
they're the basics for a prize-winning salad bowl.*

☐ Take lettuce for starters. Four main groups of its many varieties are commonly available: crisphead (notably iceberg); butterhead (including Boston and Bibb), with soft, pliable leaves; romaine (also called cos), with crisp, elongated dark leaves; and leaf lettuce (red or green), with tender "leafy" leaves that do not form heads.

☐ Then there's the endive family. It includes curly endive (sometimes miscalled chicory), a frilly, narrow-leaved, "bushy" type; escarole, a less frilly, broader-leaved variety; and Belgian or French endive, a type with narrow, blanched leaves that grow in compact, upright clusters.

☐ Now add watercress, spinach, mustard greens, celery leaves, beet tops, Chinese cabbage, nasturtium leaves and . . . and . . . and. . . .

☐ Whatever the green, it should look fresh and perky when purchased. Iceberg lettuce should be firm but resilient, "giving" slightly when squeezed. When buying butterhead and leaf lettuce, look for a bright green color (the deeper the green, the greater the vitamin A content).

☐ Store all greens in the refrigerator—in a covered container, a plastic bag or the crisper section. Watercress, parsley and fresh herbs, however, should be refrigerated in large screwtop jars. These and iceberg lettuce and romaine will keep up to a week; most other greens will droop within a few days.

☐ Wash greens several hours before using—they need time to get crisp. Wash well under running cold water, then shake off the excess moisture. To remove remaining moisture, toss in a kitchen towel or pat dry with paper towels. Return to the refrigerator.

☐ If you plan to use iceberg lettuce within a day or so, remove the core before washing. Strike the core end against a flat surface, then twist and lift out the core with your fingers. Hold the head, cored end up, under running cold water to separate and clean the leaves. Turn right side up to drain well; refrigerate in a plastic bag or in a bowl with an airtight lid.

☐ Tear (do not cut) salad greens into bite-size pieces. Exceptions? Serve iceberg lettuce cut into slices or wedges; cut Belgian endive lengthwise into quarters, crosswise into slices or simply strip off the leaves. With easily bruised butterheads, try to use the whole leaves; save the outer ones for lettuce "beds," use the small inner ones for salad.

☐ Try to use a variety of greens in tossed salads. Mix the light with the dark, the crisp with the tender. Team pale iceberg with dark-green spinach, romaine and/or curly endive. Red leaf lettuce adds color and delicate flavor. Accent with beet greens, red cabbage, fresh herbs and other "sparkers."

☐ Pour on dressing *just* before serving—using only enough to coat the leaves lightly. Toss.

GARBANZO AND ZUCCHINI TOSS

1 bunch leaf lettuce, torn into
   bite-size pieces
1 bunch romaine, torn into
   bite-size pieces
1 can (15 ounces) garbanzo beans,
   drained
2 medium zucchini, sliced
⅓ cup bottled Italian salad dressing
   Freshly ground pepper

Toss lettuce, romaine, beans, zucchini and salad dressing. Sprinkle with pepper.

10 to 12 servings.

ZUCCHINI SALAD

1 medium head iceberg lettuce, torn
   into bite-size pieces
1 small bunch romaine, torn into
   bite-size pieces
¼ cup olive oil or vegetable oil
2 medium zucchini, sliced
3 green onions, sliced
1 cup sliced radishes
3 tablespoons crumbled blue cheese
   (optional)
2 tablespoons tarragon or wine
   vinegar
¾ teaspoon salt
¼ teaspoon monosodium glutamate
1 small clove garlic, crushed
   Generous dash of pepper

Toss lettuce and romaine with oil until leaves glisten. Add zucchini, onions, radishes and cheese. Mix vinegar, salt, monosodium glutamate, garlic and pepper; toss with salad.

6 to 8 servings.

SPINACH AND SPROUTS SALAD

   Vinegar-Oil Dressing (below)
1 package (10 ounces) frozen
   Brussels sprouts
2 cups cauliflower pieces
10 ounces spinach, torn into bite-size
   pieces

Prepare Vinegar-Oil Dressing. Rinse frozen Brussels sprouts under running cold water to separate; drain. Toss Brussels sprouts and cauliflower. Pour dressing on Brussels sprouts and cauliflower. Cover and refrigerate at least 4 hours, stirring occasionally. Just before serving, toss with spinach.

6 to 8 servings.

Vinegar-Oil Dressing
⅓ cup red wine vinegar
¼ cup vegetable oil
1 tablespoon lemon juice
½ teaspoon salt
¼ teaspoon dry mustard
¼ teaspoon pepper

Shake all ingredients in tightly covered jar.
About ⅔ cup dressing.

COLOR TOSS

¾ cup mayonnaise or salad dressing
½ cup dairy sour cream
1 small head iceberg lettuce, torn
   into bite-size pieces
1 package (10 ounces) frozen green
   peas
½ cup shredded Cheddar cheese
   (about 2 ounces)
½ cup grated carrot
3 tablespoons imitation bacon
2 tablespoons chopped green onions
½ teaspoon salt

Mix mayonnaise and sour cream; toss with remaining ingredients.

8 servings.

PICKLE-CHEESE TOSS

   Pickle Dressing (below)
12 cups bite-size pieces mixed
   salad greens
 4 medium dill pickles, cut diagonally
   into slices
 8 ounces mozzarella cheese, cut
   into ⅜-inch pieces
 1 cup salted peanuts

Prepare Pickle Dressing; toss with salad greens, pickles and cheese. Sprinkle with peanuts.

12 servings.

Pickle Dressing
⅓ cup vegetable oil
3 tablespoons dill pickle juice
1 teaspoon salt
¼ teaspoon pepper

Shake all ingredients in tightly covered jar. *About ½ cup dressing.*

SPINACH-AVOCADO SALAD

   Avocado Dressing (below)
10 ounces spinach, torn into bite-size
   pieces
¼ cup toasted sesame seed (see note)
2 hard-cooked eggs, chopped
1 small onion, thinly sliced and
   separated into rings
½ avocado, cut into ½-inch pieces
1 hard-cooked egg, sliced

Prepare Avocado Dressing; toss with spinach, sesame seed, chopped eggs, onion and avocado. Garnish with egg slices.

6 to 8 servings.

Note: To toast sesame seed, heat oven to 350°. Bake in ungreased baking pan, stirring occasionally, until golden, 8 to 10 minutes.

Avocado Dressing
½ avocado
2 to 3 tablespoons lemon juice
¼ cup vegetable oil
½ teaspoon salt
   Dash of pepper

Mash avocado with lemon juice; stir in remaining ingredients. *About ⅔ cup dressing.*

HEAD-START SALAD DRESSINGS

*Take full advantage of prepared dressings but give them a hint
of "homemade." You can add that personal touch with
any of the following combinations:*

For Vegetable Salads

☐ ¼ cup oil-and-vinegar salad dressing and ¼ teaspoon chili powder

☐ ¼ cup oil-and-vinegar salad dressing and ¼ teaspoon dried oregano leaves

☐ ¼ cup oil-and-vinegar salad dressing and ¼ teaspoon ground savory

☐ ¼ cup oil-and-vinegar salad dressing and ¼ teaspoon dried thyme leaves

☐ ½ cup mayonnaise or salad dressing and ¼ cup catsup

☐ ½ cup mayonnaise or salad dressing, ¼ cup chili sauce, 1 drop red pepper sauce and dash of chili powder

☐ ½ cup mayonnaise or salad dressing and ¼ cup frozen whipped topping (thawed)

For Fruit Salads

☐ ¼ cup creamy blue cheese salad dressing and 1 tablespoon apricot preserves

☐ ¼ cup creamy blue cheese salad dressing and 2 tablespoons creamy French salad dressing

☐ ¼ cup creamy blue cheese salad dressing and ⅛ teaspoon curry powder

☐ ¼ cup fruit salad dressing and ¼ teaspoon sesame seed

☐ ¼ cup French salad dressing and ⅛ teaspoon celery seed

☐ ½ cup mayonnaise or salad dressing, 2 tablespoons cranberry juice cocktail and ¼ teaspoon poppy seed

BANANA-SPINACH TOSS

2 tablespoons butter or margarine,
  softened
2 firm medium bananas, thinly sliced
  Salt
  Banana–Poppy Seed Dressing (below)
5 ounces spinach, torn into bite-size
  pieces

Heat oven to 350°. Brush bottom of jelly roll pan, 15½x10½x1 inch, with butter. Spread banana slices in single layer in pan; sprinkle with salt. Bake uncovered until golden brown and crisp, 25 to 30 minutes. Immediately remove from pan; drain on paper towels.

Prepare Banana–Poppy Seed Dressing; toss with spinach and bananas.

4 servings.

Banana–Poppy Seed Dressing
½ medium banana, mashed
2 tablespoons vegetable oil
1 tablespoon lemon juice
1½ teaspoons sugar
¼ teaspoon dry mustard
⅛ teaspoon salt
1½ teaspoons poppy seed

Mix banana, oil, lemon juice, sugar, mustard and salt. Stir in poppy seed. *About ½ cup dressing.*

ENDIVE-FRUIT SALAD

  Mallow Dressing (below)
½ bunch curly endive, torn into
  bite-size pieces
1 package (about 10 ounces) frozen
  melon balls, partially thawed and
  drained, or 1 cup fresh melon balls
2 apples, chopped

Prepare Mallow Dressing; toss with remaining ingredients.

8 servings.

Mallow Dressing
½ cup marshmallow crème
1 tablespoon plus 1½ teaspoons
  orange juice
2 tablespoons mayonnaise or salad
  dressing
⅛ teaspoon salt

Beat marshmallow crème and orange juice. Stir in mayonnaise and salt. *About ½ cup dressing.*

MANDARIN SALAD

¼ cup sliced almonds
1 tablespoon plus 1 teaspoon sugar
  Mandarin Dressing (below)
¼ medium head iceberg lettuce
¼ medium bunch romaine
2 medium stalks celery, chopped
2 green onions (with tops), thinly sliced
1 can (11 ounces) mandarin orange segments, drained

Cook almonds and sugar over low heat, stirring constantly, until sugar is melted and almonds are coated. Cool and break apart.

Prepare Mandarin Dressing. Tear lettuce and romaine into bite-size pieces; toss with dressing, celery, onions, orange segments and almonds.

4 to 6 servings.

Mandarin Dressing
¼ cup vegetable oil
2 tablespoons sugar
2 tablespoons vinegar
1 tablespoon snipped parsley
½ teaspoon salt
  Dash of pepper
  Dash of red pepper sauce

Shake all ingredients in tightly covered jar. *About ⅓ cup dressing.*

SUNNY CITRUS SALAD

  Blue Cheese–Lemon Dressing (below)
1 small clove garlic, cut into halves
2 medium grapefruit, pared and sectioned
1 small head iceberg lettuce, torn into bite-size pieces
1 small bunch curly endive, romaine or chicory, torn into bite-size pieces
1 can (11 ounces) mandarin orange segments, drained
1 jar (2 ounces) sliced pimiento, drained
¼ teaspoon salt
  Freshly ground pepper

Prepare Blue Cheese–Lemon Dressing. Rub large salad bowl with cut clove of garlic. Place grapefruit sections, lettuce, endive, orange segments and pimiento in bowl; sprinkle with salt. Toss with dressing; sprinkle with pepper.

8 to 10 servings.

Blue Cheese–Lemon Dressing
¼ cup crumbled blue cheese (about 1 ounce)
¼ cup vegetable oil
⅓ cup dairy sour cream
1 tablespoon lemon juice
¼ teaspoon grated lemon peel
¼ teaspoon garlic salt
¼ teaspoon salt
  Dash of monosodium glutamate

Mash cheese with fork. Stir in oil; beat until mixture is smooth. Stir in remaining ingredients. Cover and refrigerate at least 1 hour. *About ¾ cup dressing.*

Tossed greens — but with a difference. Clockwise from top left: Antipasto Toss (page 20), Fantastic Green Salad (page 8), Watercress and Asparagus Toss (page 10).

Flaming Spinach Salad (page 9) — sure to impress. Ignite the brandy and toss the salad at the table.

GRAPE-PEA SALAD

Creamy Oil Dressing (below)
½ head iceberg lettuce, torn into
bite-size pieces
½ medium head red or green
cabbage, coarsely shredded
1 cup fresh green peas or frozen
green peas, thawed and drained
1 cup seedless green grapes

Prepare Creamy Oil Dressing; toss with remaining ingredients.

5 or 6 servings.

Creamy Oil Dressing
2 tablespoons vegetable oil
1 tablespoon red wine vinegar
1 teaspoon mayonnaise or salad
dressing
¼ teaspoon salt
⅛ teaspoon lemon pepper
Dash of paprika

Shake all ingredients in tightly covered jar.
¼ cup dressing.

ORANGE TOSS

2 cans (11 ounces each) mandarin
orange segments, drained
½ small head iceberg lettuce,
coarsely shredded
2 green onions, thinly sliced
Bottled sweet-and-sour salad dressing

Reserve 4 orange segments. Toss remaining segments with lettuce. Divide lettuce mixture among 4 salad bowls; sprinkle with sliced onions. Garnish each salad with reserved orange segment; drizzle small amount salad dressing over each salad.

4 servings.

MINTED PINEAPPLE TOSS

Citrus Dressing (below)
½ head iceberg lettuce, torn into
bite-size pieces
¼ bunch curly endive, torn into
bite-size pieces
1 can (13¼ ounces) pineapple chunks,
drained
½ medium green pepper, chopped
1 large stalk celery, chopped
¼ cup toasted broken walnuts
(see note)
2 teaspoons snipped mint leaves

Prepare Citrus Dressing; toss with lettuce, endive, pineapple, green pepper, celery and walnuts. Garnish with mint leaves.

6 servings.

Note: To toast walnuts, heat oven to 350°. Bake in ungreased baking pan, stirring occasionally, until golden, about 10 minutes.

Citrus Dressing
¼ cup vegetable oil
2 tablespoons orange marmalade
2 tablespoons lemon juice
¾ teaspoon salt
Dash of pepper
Dash of red pepper sauce

Shake all ingredients in tightly covered jar.
½ cup dressing.

ANTIPASTO TOSS

Pictured on page 17.

1 can (15 ounces) garbanzo beans, drained
1 jar (about 7 ounces) marinated artichoke hearts
¼ cup pitted ripe olives, drained and sliced
½ cup bottled herb-and-garlic or Italian salad dressing
2 bunches romaine, torn into bite-size pieces
1 bunch leaf lettuce, torn into bite-size pieces
2 hard-cooked eggs, sliced
½ cup sliced pepperoni
Freshly ground pepper

Toss beans, artichoke hearts (with liquid), olives and salad dressing. Top with romaine and lettuce. Arrange eggs and pepperoni on salad greens; sprinkle with pepper. Cover and refrigerate no longer than 4 hours. Toss just before serving.

8 servings.

GLOSSY RED, WHITE AND GREEN SALAD

Cocktail Sauce (below)
4 ounces spinach, torn into bite-size pieces
1 can (4½ ounces) small shrimp, drained
4 ounces mushrooms, sliced
1 cup cauliflowerets, cut into ½-inch pieces

Prepare Cocktail Sauce; toss with remaining ingredients.

6 servings.

Cocktail Sauce
½ cup chili sauce
1 teaspoon prepared horseradish
1 teaspoon lemon juice
¼ teaspoon Worcestershire sauce
Dash of salt
Dash of pepper

Shake all ingredients in tightly covered jar.
½ cup dressing.

SHRIMP COCKTAIL TOSS

Toss about 6 ounces spinach, torn into bite-size pieces, with 1 jar (about 4 ounces) shrimp cocktail.°

6 servings.

°1 can (4½ ounces) small shrimp, drained, and ¼ cup cocktail sauce can be substituted for the shrimp cocktail.

Note: For a two-tone salad, use half Bibb lettuce and half spinach.

FRUIT SALADS

Stand-out Attractions to Brighten Your Table

Splashy reds, glistening yellows and oranges,
soft colors, bold colors — almost reason enough to serve these salads.
But pretty as they are, fruit salads offer a wealth of other good things:
texture contrasts, from juicy lushness to solid crunchiness;
taste contrasts, from sweet to tart. And, naturally, literally an
orchard of vitamins and minerals. For you and others,
there are hardly any salads more rewarding than
these appetite teasers and pleasers.

APPLE-CHEESE WEDGES

⅓ cup pasteurized process smoky-
   flavored cheese spread
1 tablespoon finely chopped walnuts
2 apples, cut into wedges
   Salad greens

Mix cheese and walnuts. Spread 1 side of
each apple wedge with cheese mixture.
Put wedges together to make 4 apple halves.
Serve each apple half rounded side up on
salad greens.

4 servings.

WALDORF SALADS

2 medium apples, coarsely chopped
2 stalks celery, chopped
⅓ cup coarsely chopped walnuts
½ cup mayonnaise or salad dressing
4 to 6 lettuce cups
   Apple slices

Mix chopped apples, celery, walnuts and
mayonnaise. Spoon salad into lettuce cups.
Garnish with apple slices.

4 to 6 servings.

VARIATIONS

Curried Waldorf Salads: Stir ½ teaspoon
curry powder into the mayonnaise.

Maple Nut Waldorf Salads: Stir ½ teaspoon
maple flavoring and ¼ teaspoon ground
cinnamon into the mayonnaise.

Molasses Waldorf Salads: Stir 1 tablespoon
molasses into the mayonnaise.

Peanut Butter Waldorf Salads: Decrease
mayonnaise to ⅓ cup and stir in ¼ cup
crunchy peanut butter. Substitute peanuts
for the walnuts.

MOONGLOW APRICOT SALAD

1 can (17 ounces) apricot halves,
   drained (reserve 1 teaspoon syrup)
1 package (3 ounces) cream cheese,
   softened
¼ cup cut-up dates
⅛ teaspoon ground ginger
⅓ cup finely chopped pecans
   Lettuce leaves

Mix reserved apricot syrup, the cream
cheese, dates and ginger. Drop mixture by
teaspoonfuls into pecans; roll around to coat
completely. Shape into about 1-inch balls.
Place 1 ball in each apricot half; arrange
on lettuce.

4 servings.

CHERRY-GRAPE SALADS

1 can (16 ounces) pitted dark sweet
   cherries, drained
1 can (8¾ ounces) seedless green
   grapes, drained
1 carton (8 ounces) unflavored yogurt
1 cup flaked coconut
1 cup miniature marshmallows
6 lettuce cups

Mix cherries, grapes, yogurt, coconut and
marshmallows. Cover and refrigerate at
least 4 hours. Spoon salad into lettuce cups.

6 servings.

ORANGE-ONION SALADS

Ruby Blue Cheese Dressing (below)
3 medium oranges, pared and sliced
½ medium Bermuda onion, thinly
   sliced
   Curly endive

Prepare Ruby Blue Cheese Dressing. Arrange 3 orange slices and 1 onion slice on endive on each of 6 salad plates; drizzle 2 to 3 tablespoons dressing over each salad.

6 servings.

Ruby Blue Cheese Dressing
⅔ cup crumbled blue cheese (about
   3 ounces)
½ cup vegetable oil
⅓ cup catsup
3 tablespoons vinegar
1 tablespoon finely chopped onion
½ teaspoon salt
½ teaspoon pepper
½ teaspoon dry mustard
½ teaspoon paprika

Shake all ingredients in tightly covered jar. Refrigerate at least 3 hours. Shake before serving. *About 1 cup dressing.*

GRAPEFRUIT-ORANGE SALADS

1 grapefruit, pared and sectioned
1 can (11 ounces) mandarin orange
   segments, drained
1 cup bite-size pieces lettuce
¼ cup chopped celery
¼ cup mayonnaise or salad
   dressing
½ teaspoon instant minced onion
½ teaspoon lemon juice or vinegar
¼ teaspoon celery seed
   Dash of salt
5 lettuce cups
   Pomegranate seeds or chopped
   pimiento

Cut grapefruit sections into halves. Toss with orange segments, lettuce, celery, mayonnaise, onion, lemon juice, celery seed and salt. Spoon salad into lettuce cups; sprinkle with pomegranate seeds.

5 servings.

SHADY GLADE SALAD

   No-Oil Dressing (below)
3 medium oranges, pared, sliced
    and cut into halves
5 medium radishes, sliced
2 stalks celery, cut diagonally
    into slices
3 green onions, sliced
1 medium green pepper, cut into
    1-inch strips
1 medium cucumber, sliced

Prepare No-Oil Dressing; pour on remaining ingredients in shallow glass or plastic dish. Cover and refrigerate at least 1 hour. Drain salad before serving.

8 servings.

No-Oil Dressing
⅔ cup water
½ cup sugar
⅓ cup vinegar
½ teaspoon salt
¼ teaspoon pepper

Shake all ingredients in tightly covered jar. *About 1⅓ cups dressing.*

PEACH SALADS

⅓ cup cut-up dried prunes
6 peach halves
    Salad greens
3 tablespoons slivered almonds
1 teaspoon grated lemon peel
1 cup frozen whipped topping, thawed
1 tablespoon slivered almonds

Place prunes in jar. Pour enough boiling water on prunes to cover. Cover and refrigerate at least 24 hours.

Arrange peach halves on salad greens. Stir prunes, 3 tablespoons almonds and the lemon peel into whipped topping. Spoon topping mixture onto peach halves. Garnish with 1 tablespoon almonds.

6 servings.

FRESH PEACH AND PEAR SALADS

1 package (3¾ ounces) vanilla instant
    pudding and pie filling
½ cup milk
⅓ cup dairy sour cream
1 package (10 ounces) frozen
    raspberries, thawed and drained
    (reserve syrup)
6 peaches, sliced
6 pears, sliced
    Leaf lettuce

Beat pudding and pie filling (dry), milk, sour cream and reserved raspberry syrup until smooth. Reserve 8 raspberries; fold remaining raspberries into pudding mixture. Refrigerate at least 1 hour.

Fold peaches and pears into raspberry mixture. Spoon salad onto lettuce and garnish with reserved raspberries.

8 servings.

PEACH SALADS WITH MOLASSES CREAM

Molasses Cream (below)
6 peaches, cut into halves°
Leaf lettuce
3 tablespoons chopped nuts

Prepare Molasses Cream. Place peach halves cut sides up on lettuce; sprinkle with nuts. Top with Molasses Cream.

6 servings.

°12 canned peach halves, well drained, can be substituted for the fresh peaches.

Molasses Cream
Mix ½ cup frozen whipped topping, thawed, and 1 teaspoon molasses. *About ½ cup dressing.*

HULA SALADS

1 cup creamed cottage cheese
3 tablespoons raisins, nuts or cut-up dates
Salad greens
1 can (8¼ ounces) sliced pineapple, drained
Flaked or shredded coconut
4 maraschino cherries

Mix cottage cheese and raisins. Spoon ¼ cup of the cottage cheese–raisin mixture onto salad greens on each of 4 salad plates. Top with pineapple slice; sprinkle with coconut. Place cherry in center of each pineapple slice.

4 servings.

BURMESE RICE-FRUIT SALAD

1 can (13¼ ounces) crushed pineapple, drained
1 cup chilled cooked rice
½ cup flaked coconut
¼ cup golden raisins
½ cup chilled whipping cream
2 tablespoons sugar
½ teaspoon vanilla
½ teaspoon almond extract
¼ teaspoon ground ginger
Dash of salt
3 tablespoons slivered almonds
Salad greens
1 tablespoon slivered almonds

Mix pineapple, rice, coconut and raisins. Beat cream, sugar, vanilla, almond extract, ginger and salt in chilled small mixer bowl until stiff; fold into rice mixture. Stir in 3 tablespoons slivered almonds. Spoon salad onto salad greens and garnish with 1 tablespoon slivered almonds.

4 to 6 servings.

PINEAPPLE FRUIT SALAD

1 pineapple
1 cup pitted dark sweet cherries
1 cup cantaloupe or other melon balls
Fluffy Coconut Mayonnaise (below)

Cut pineapple lengthwise into halves through green top. Cut out pineapple, leaving ½-inch walls. Cut pineapple into bite-size pieces, removing any eyes and fibrous core. Mix pineapple pieces, cherries and cantaloupe balls; spoon into pineapple shells. Cover and refrigerate at least 1 hour.

Prepare Fluffy Coconut Mayonnaise; serve with salad.

4 to 6 servings.

Fluffy Coconut Mayonnaise
Mix 1½ cups frozen whipped topping, thawed, and ⅓ cup mayonnaise or salad dressing. Top with ¼ cup toasted flaked coconut (see note). *About 1⅓ cups dressing.*

Note: To toast coconut, heat oven to 350°. Bake in ungreased baking pan, stirring occasionally, until golden, 5 to 7 minutes.

PINK PINEAPPLE-BEET SALADS

1 jar (16 ounces) pickled beets, drained and chopped
1 can (13¼ ounces) pineapple chunks, drained
1 cup flaked coconut
1 cup miniature marshmallows
1 cup dairy sour cream
6 lettuce cups

Mix beets, pineapple, coconut, marshmallows and sour cream. Cover and refrigerate at least 4 hours. Spoon salad into lettuce cups.

6 servings.

MACARONI-PINEAPPLE TOSS

1 package (7 ounces) elbow macaroni
2 cans (20 ounces each) crushed pineapple, drained
1 cup shredded Cheddar cheese (about 4 ounces)
1 large stalk celery, chopped
¾ cup mayonnaise or salad dressing
⅓ cup quartered maraschino cherries

Cook macaroni as directed on package; drain. Rinse with cold water. Toss with remaining ingredients. Cover and refrigerate at least 1 hour.

6 servings.

24-HOUR SALAD

Old-fashioned Fruit Dressing (below)
1 can (17 ounces) dark sweet cherries, drained
2 cans (13¼ ounces each) pineapple chunks, drained (reserve 2 tablespoons syrup)
3 oranges, pared, sectioned and cut up
1 cup miniature marshmallows

Prepare Old-fashioned Fruit Dressing. Mix fruits and marshmallows; toss with dressing. Cover and refrigerate at least 12 hours.

8 to 10 servings.

Old-fashioned Fruit Dressing
2 eggs, beaten
2 tablespoons sugar
2 tablespoons vinegar or lemon juice
2 tablespoons reserved pineapple syrup
1 tablespoon butter or margarine
Dash of salt
¾ cup chilled whipping cream

Heat eggs, sugar, vinegar, pineapple syrup, butter and salt just to boiling, stirring constantly. Remove from heat; cool. Beat cream in chilled small mixer bowl until stiff. Fold egg mixture into whipped cream. *About 2 cups dressing.*

WINTER FRUIT SALAD
Pictured on page 35.

Honey-Lime Dressing (below) or lime-flavored yogurt
1 avocado, cut into ¼-inch slices
Lemon juice
Salt
1 grapefruit, pared and sectioned°
1 apple, cut into ¼-inch slices°
Spinach leaves
½ cup whole cranberry sauce

Prepare Honey-Lime Dressing. Sprinkle avocado slices with lemon juice and salt. Arrange avocado slices, grapefruit sections and apple slices in circle on spinach leaves. Spoon cranberry sauce into center. Serve with dressing.

4 servings.

°2 oranges and 2 bananas can be substituted for the grapefruit and apple.

Honey-Lime Dressing
2 tablespoons honey
2 tablespoons vegetable oil
2 tablespoons frozen limeade concentrate, thawed
¼ teaspoon celery seed

Mix all ingredients until smooth. *About ⅓ cup dressing.*

FRUIT SALADS   27

TROPICAL AND EXOTIC FRUITS

Add a touch of the tropics to your fruit bowls and salads—no matter where you live. In today's markets, the world is virtually at your fingertips. But how and what to buy?

☐ Avocados will be unblemished if you anticipate their use by several days and buy firm ones. Let ripen at room temperature; when they yield to gentle pressure, they're ready to eat or to store in the refrigerator, where they'll keep for several days. Halved lengthwise and pitted, avocados serve as edible salad bowls; pared and sliced or cut up, they are added to the salad. To prepare an avocado, cut lengthwise, right around the hard center seed. Rotate the halves in opposite directions to help separate. If the seed won't dislodge, whack it with a sharp knife, twist the knife and lift out the seed. Strip off the avocado skin or, if necessary, pare. Sprinkle cut avocados with lemon or lime juice—the flesh discolors easily. Store an unused half, with the pit still in, closely wrapped in a plastic bag. To mash avocados, use a fork, sieve, blender or food mill.

☐ Bananas ripen better off the plant than on it. Select slightly green fruit and allow to mature as a cheerful centerpiece. When you think the ripening has gone far enough, ignore that popular jingle and refrigerate. The skins may blacken, but the flesh will keep for several days.

☐ The egg-shaped kiwi fruit of New Zealand hides a luscious green under its drab brown exterior. Let ripen at room temperature until soft, then refrigerate. Once peeled, the whole fruit is edible.

☐ Mangoes vary in size and shape. Allow to ripen at room temperature until the flesh yields to gentle pressure and any green is largely background color, then refrigerate. To prepare, score the tough skin in 4 to 6 sections, piercing it with a paring knife; strip the skin away and cut the fruit into slices.

☐ Papayas look like pear-shaped melons, but they grow on trees, not vines. If purchased when green, let ripen at room temperature for 3 to 5 days. When yellow-orange, refrigerate for use within 1 week. Prepare and serve just as you would cantaloupe.

☐ Pineapples don't ripen after picking. Try for one that has an aroma, no soft spots and a spirited green crown. Refrigerate if not using immediately. To prepare a pineapple for use, carefully twist out the green top; cut pineapple into halves, then quarters. Slice the fruit from the rind. Cut off the core and remove any "eyes."

☐ You don't eat pomegranates; you eat their fleshy red seeds, which may be frozen almost indefinitely. Select large red to purple fruits, heavy for their size, with tough skins. To prepare, cut lengthwise and remove the seeds with a spoon. Or score lengthwise in several places and soak in cold water 5 minutes; then break apart under water, separating the seeds from the pulp. Skim off the pulp and drain seeds. Scatter a few on a fruit salad to dazzle the diners.

TROPICAL FRUIT SALAD

Pictured on page 36.

Almond Dressing (below)
3 bananas, sliced
2 avocados, sliced
2 kiwi fruit, sliced
1 mango, cut up
1 papaya, sliced
¼ cup toasted flaked coconut

Prepare Almond Dressing. Mix bananas, avocados, kiwi, mango and papaya; sprinkle with coconut. Serve with dressing.

8 servings.

Almond Dressing
⅓ cup toasted chopped almonds
⅓ cup orange juice
⅓ cup vegetable oil
3 tablespoons packed brown sugar
2 tablespoons light rum
¼ teaspoon salt
¼ teaspoon paprika

Shake all ingredients in tightly covered jar. Refrigerate at least 1 hour. *About 1 cup dressing.*

STARBURST FRUIT SALAD

Peanut Dressing (right)
6 medium romaine leaves
3 small bananas
¼ cup chopped salted peanuts
1 can (13¼ ounces) pineapple chunks, drained
1 can (11 ounces) mandarin orange segments, drained
1 cup strawberries

Prepare Peanut Dressing. Arrange romaine leaves in starburst pattern on large serving plate. Cut bananas lengthwise into halves.

Place 1 banana half, cut side down, in center of each romaine leaf; sprinkle with peanuts. Arrange pineapple chunks and orange segments alternately between banana halves. Place strawberries in center of starburst. Serve salad with dressing.

6 servings.

Peanut Dressing
¼ cup honey
¼ cup creamy peanut butter
1 tablespoon lemon juice

Mix all ingredients. *½ cup dressing.*

CANNED FRUIT SALAD PLATE

Cheese Dressing (below)
1 can (16 ounces) pitted dark sweet cherries, chilled and drained
1 can (14 ounces) spiced red apple rings, chilled and drained
1 can (11 ounces) mandarin orange segments, chilled and drained
1 can (8¾ ounces) sliced pears, chilled and drained
1 cup pecan halves
Salad greens

Prepare Cheese Dressing. Arrange cherries, apple rings, orange segments, pear slices and pecan halves on salad greens around bowl of dressing.

6 servings.

Cheese Dressing
1 cup shredded Cheddar cheese (about 4 ounces)
½ cup mayonnaise or salad dressing
½ cup dairy sour cream
¼ teaspoon red pepper sauce

Mix all ingredients. *About 1½ cups dressing.*

SUMMER FRUIT BOWL

Pictured on page 35.

2 peaches, cut up
1 cup blueberries
1 cup melon balls
1 cup sliced strawberries
1 cup seedless green grapes
3 tablespoons orange-flavored
   liqueur or orange juice
⅔ cup dairy sour cream
3 tablespoons packed brown sugar
   Brown sugar

Toss peaches, blueberries, melon balls, strawberries, grapes and liqueur. Mix sour cream and 3 tablespoons brown sugar; sprinkle with additional brown sugar. Serve fruit mixture with sour cream dressing.

6 servings.

FRESH FRUIT ON CRISPY NOODLES

   Curry Dressing (below)
3 bananas, sliced
2 pears, cut up
2 peaches, sliced
2 cups pitted dark sweet cherries
1 can (8 ounces) crushed pineapple in
   juice, drained (reserve 2
   tablespoons juice)
2 cups chow mein noodles

Prepare Curry Dressing. Toss bananas, pears, peaches, cherries and pineapple. Arrange ⅓ cup chow mein noodles on each of 6 salad plates; top with fruit mixture. Serve with dressing.

6 servings.

Curry Dressing

½ cup dairy sour cream
2 tablespoons reserved pineapple
   juice
1 tablespoon honey
½ teaspoon curry powder

Mix all ingredients. *About ⅔ cup dressing.*

STRAWBERRY-RHUBARB MOLD

1 package (20 ounces) frozen unsweetened rhubarb
1 package (3 ounces) strawberry-flavored gelatin
1 or 2 drops red food color (optional)
1 can (8 ounces) crushed pineapple in juice
¼ cup chopped nuts
  Crushed Pineapple Dressing (below)
  Salad greens

Prepare Rhubarb Sauce as directed on package of frozen rhubarb; remove from heat. Stir in gelatin and food color. Refrigerate until very thick, about 1½ hours.

Reserve 2 tablespoons pineapple for Crushed Pineapple Dressing. Stir remaining pineapple (with juice) and nuts into gelatin mixture; pour into 4-cup mold. Refrigerate until firm, at least 4 hours.

Prepare Crushed Pineapple Dressing. Unmold salad on salad greens and serve with dressing.

6 servings.

Crushed Pineapple Dressing
½ cup frozen whipped topping, thawed
¼ cup mayonnaise or salad dressing
2 tablespoons reserved crushed pineapple

Mix all ingredients. *About ⅔ cup dressing.*

CHERRY-BERRY SALADS

1 cup boiling water
1 package (6 ounces) orange-flavored gelatin
2 cups strawberries, sliced
1 banana, sliced
1 can (21 ounces) cherry pie filling
1 teaspoon lemon juice
  Orange Topping (below)

Pour boiling water on gelatin in bowl; stir until gelatin is dissolved. Stir in strawberries, banana, pie filling and lemon juice. Pour into baking pan, 9x9x2 inches. Refrigerate until firm. Prepare Orange Topping; serve with salad.

8 or 9 servings.

Orange Topping
Mix 1 carton (8 ounces) dairy sour cream and 3 tablespoons orange marmalade. *About 1 cup topping.*

BERRY-WINE SALAD

1 cup boiling water
1 package (3 ounces) strawberry-flavored gelatin
1 package (10 ounces) frozen sliced strawberries, partially thawed
1 cup seedless green grapes
⅔ cup sweet white wine
  Salad greens
1 carton (8 ounces) strawberry-flavored yogurt

Pour boiling water on gelatin in bowl; stir until gelatin is dissolved. Stir in strawberries; break apart with fork. Stir in 1 cup grapes and the wine. Pour into 4-cup mold. Refrigerate until firm. Unmold on salad greens and serve with yogurt.

6 to 8 servings.

MOLDED SALADS

All-American beauties—these remarkably versatile salads may be made 2 to 3 days in advance. Perfect for do-aheaders.

☐ Almost anything that doesn't leak can be used as a salad mold, but the gelatin will thicken and firm more quickly in containers of thin metal, such as ice cube trays or stainless steel bowls. (Salads will unmold more easily, too.) A collection of pretty copper molds in varying sizes, however, leads to spectacular salads . . . and handsomely decorated kitchen walls.

☐ If you don't know the size of your mold, fill it with water and then measure the contents. If you want to use a 4-cup mold but have a 6-cup recipe, use the recipe as is. Don't try to adapt a gelatin recipe with partial amounts. The extra gelatin can be poured into individual molds or custard cups and used to accent other meals or for between-meal snacks.

☐ Follow recipe directions exactly when dissolving gelatin. Flavored and unflavored gelatins are dissolved by different methods.

☐ When adding solids, first thicken the gelatin mixture until it mounds slightly when dropped from a spoon. If you're in a hurry, place the mixture in a bowl of ice and water or in the freezer compartment instead of the refrigerator. If the gelatin becomes too firm, soften over hot water. When the mixture has thickened, fold in the solids. (Drain fruits and vegetables thoroughly to avoid diluting the gelatin.)

☐ To design a patterned mold, either arrange the solids in the bottom of your mold and carefully spoon the thickened gelatin over them, or first spoon a little thickened gelatin into the bottom of the mold and then arrange your solids in an attractive pattern. Allow each layer to become firm before proceeding with the next. For a dramatic effect, make each layer a different jewel-like color.

☐ To unmold, dip the mold in warm, not hot, water to the depth of its contents; carefully loosen the edge of the salad with the tip of a paring knife. Place a chilled serving plate on top of the mold and, holding tightly, invert both plate and mold as a unit. Shake— and plop, your salad is unmolded. If there is no plop, repeat the process. And again, if necessary. With large and multi-grooved molds, you may find it easier to first invert the mold on a chilled plate. Then press a well-wrung-out hot kitchen towel all over the mold and into the depressions until you hear the plop. Repeat if necessary.

STRAWBERRY FREEZE

1 quart strawberry ice cream
1 can (13¼ ounces) crushed
    pineapple, drained
1 carton (4½ ounces) frozen whipped
    topping, thawed
1 jar (4 ounces) maraschino cherries,
    drained and cut into halves
1 package (3 ounces) cream cheese,
    cut into ½-inch cubes
1 banana, sliced

Soften ice cream until consistency of whipped cream. Fold pineapple, whipped topping, cherries, cream cheese and banana into ice cream. Spread in ungreased baking pan, 13x9x2 inches. Freeze until firm, at least 3 hours.

15 servings.

RASPBERRY-PEACH SALADS

1 cup boiling water
1 package (6 ounces) raspberry-
    flavored gelatin
1 package (12 ounces) frozen
    raspberries
1 can (21 ounces) peach pie filling
1 teaspoon lemon juice
    Peach Topping (below)

Pour boiling water on gelatin in bowl; stir until gelatin is dissolved. Stir in frozen raspberries, pie filling and lemon juice. Pour into baking pan, 9x9x2 inches. Refrigerate until firm. Prepare Peach Topping; serve with salads.

8 or 9 servings.

Peach Topping
Mix 1 carton (8 ounces) unflavored yogurt and 3 tablespoons peach preserves. *About 1 cup topping.*

PASTEL FRUIT RING MOLD

2½ cups boiling water
1 package (6 ounces) cherry-flavored
    gelatin°
1 can (6 ounces) frozen lemonade
    concentrate
1 carton (9 ounces) frozen whipped
    topping, thawed
    Salad greens
1 pint raspberries°

Pour boiling water on gelatin in bowl; stir until gelatin is dissolved. Stir in frozen concentrate. Refrigerate until slightly thickened, about 1 hour 15 minutes.

Stir whipped topping into gelatin mixture; beat on low speed until light and fluffy, about 1 minute. Pour into 8-cup ring mold. Refrigerate until firm, at least 4 hours. Unmold on salad greens and fill center of salad with raspberries.

12 servings.

°Your favorite flavor gelatin and fruit can be substituted for the cherry-flavored gelatin and the raspberries.

FROSTED APRICOT SALAD

2 cups boiling water
1 package (6 ounces) orange-flavored gelatin
1 can (17 ounces) apricot halves
1 can (8¼ ounces) crushed pineapple
⅔ cup chopped pecans
2 large bananas
1 cup chilled whipping cream
1 package (3 ounces) cream cheese, softened
2 tablespoons powdered sugar
½ teaspoon almond extract
2 tablespoons flaked coconut

Pour boiling water on gelatin in bowl; stir until gelatin is dissolved. Stir in apricots (with syrup), pineapple (with syrup) and pecans. Refrigerate until slightly thickened, about 1½ hours.

Slice bananas; stir into gelatin mixture. Pour into baking dish or pan, 9x9x2 inches. Refrigerate until firm, at least 4 hours.

Beat cream in chilled small mixer bowl until stiff; beat in cream cheese, sugar and extract until mixture is smooth. Spread over gelatin; sprinkle with coconut.

8 or 9 servings.

WATERMELON MOLD

2 envelopes unflavored gelatin
3½ cups watermelon puree (see note)
¼ cup sugar
¼ cup fresh lemon juice
¼ teaspoon salt
½ package (8-ounce size) cream cheese, softened
⅓ cup mayonnaise or salad dressing
1 tablespoon milk
Few drops green food color
Mint leaves
Watermelon balls

Sprinkle gelatin on 1 cup of the watermelon puree in saucepan to soften; stir in sugar. Stir over low heat until gelatin is dissolved. Remove from heat; stir remaining puree into gelatin mixture. Stir in lemon juice and salt; pour into 1-quart bowl. Refrigerate until firm, at least 8 hours. Stir gently during first hour to prevent separation.

Unmold watermelon on serving plate. Beat cream cheese, mayonnaise and milk until smooth; stir in food color. Frost mold with cream cheese mixture. Garnish with mint leaves and watermelon balls.

8 servings.

Note: To make puree, cut watermelon into pieces; remove seeds and rind. Place 3 cups melon pieces in blender container. Cover and blend until pureed, about 15 seconds. Repeat until desired amount of puree is obtained. Four pounds watermelon will yield about 3½ cups puree.

Fruit salads for any season: Winter Fruit Salad (page 27) in back, Summer Fruit Bowl (page 30) in front.

Tropical Fruit Salad (page 29). This exotic conversation-maker calls for avocados, bananas, papayas, mangoes and kiwis, a sprinkling of toasted coconut and a zesty Almond Dressing.

A salad on the side? Here are four excellent suggestions. Clockwise from top left: Picnic Tomatoes (page 46), Corny Coleslaw (page 43), Eight-Vegetable Marinade (page 47), Potato-Broccoli Salad (page 48).

Shapely do-ahead salads: Confetti Soufflé (page 52) in back, Avocado Molded Crown (page 50) in front.

CHERRY-PINEAPPLE SALAD

1 cup boiling water
1 package (3 ounces) cherry-flavored gelatin
¾ cup dairy sour cream
½ cup mayonnaise or salad dressing
2 teaspoons prepared horseradish
1 can (8¼ ounces) crushed pineapple, drained (reserve syrup)
½ cup chopped nuts
 Salad greens
 Black cherries or raspberries

Pour boiling water on gelatin in blender container. Cover and blend on low speed until gelatin is dissolved, about 10 seconds. Add sour cream, mayonnaise, horseradish and reserved pineapple syrup. Cover and blend on low speed 20 seconds. Stir in pineapple and nuts; pour into 4-cup mold. Refrigerate until firm, at least 4 hours. Unmold on salad greens and garnish with cherries.

6 servings.

VARIATION

Orange-Apricot Salad: Substitute orange-flavored gelatin for the cherry-flavored gelatin and 1 can (8¾ ounces) apricot halves for the pineapple. Do not stir apricot halves into gelatin mixture. Refrigerate gelatin mixture in bowl until slightly thickened. Arrange apricot halves cut sides up in mold. Pour gelatin mixture on apricots. Refrigerate until firm, at least 4 hours.

BLACK CHERRY MOLD

1 can (16 ounces) pitted dark sweet cherries, drained (reserve ¾ cup syrup)
¾ cup water or dry red wine
1 package (6 ounces) black cherry–flavored gelatin
1¾ cups ginger ale
1 package (3 ounces) slivered almonds (optional)
 Salad greens
1 carton (8 ounces) black cherry–flavored yogurt

Heat reserved cherry syrup and water to boiling; pour on gelatin in bowl. Stir until gelatin is dissolved. Stir in ginger ale. Refrigerate until slightly thickened.

Stir cherries and almonds into gelatin mixture; pour into 6-cup mold. Refrigerate until firm, at least 2 hours. Unmold on salad greens and serve with yogurt.

8 to 10 servings.

PINEAPPLE-BLUEBERRY SQUARES

2 cups boiling water
1 package (6 ounces) raspberry-flavored gelatin
1 can (16 ounces) blueberries, drained (reserve ⅔ cup syrup)
1 can (8¼ ounces) crushed pineapple
1 package (8 ounces) cream cheese, softened
½ cup dairy sour cream
¼ cup sugar
  Chopped nuts

Pour boiling water on gelatin in bowl; stir until gelatin is dissolved. Stir in blueberries, reserved blueberry syrup and the pineapple (with syrup). Pour into baking dish or pan, 8x8x2 inches. Refrigerate until firm, at least 4 hours.

Mix cream cheese, sour cream and sugar. Spread over gelatin; sprinkle with nuts. Cut into squares.

9 servings.

ORANGE-BUTTERMILK SALAD

1 cup boiling water
1 package (6 ounces) orange-flavored gelatin
1 cup vanilla ice cream
1 cup buttermilk
1 can (11 ounces) mandarin orange segments, drained
  Lemon–Sour Cream Dressing (below)
  Curly endive

Pour boiling water on gelatin in bowl; stir until gelatin is dissolved. Stir in ice cream until mixture is smooth. Stir in buttermilk and orange segments; pour into 5-cup mold. Refrigerate until firm, at least 4 hours.

Prepare Lemon–Sour Cream Dressing. Unmold salad on endive; serve with dressing.

8 to 10 servings.

Lemon–Sour Cream Dressing
½ cup dairy sour cream
1 tablespoon packed brown sugar
1 tablespoon sunflower nuts
1 teaspoon grated lemon peel

Mix all ingredients. *About ½ cup dressing.*

VEGETABLE SALADS

Sprightly Besides to Balance Your Menu

Seasonings and such can make a vegetable do perk-ups.
Then again, in combinations of twos, threes, fours and mores, they
can make you forget that vegetables were ever supposed to be dull.
These garden friends are in the best of company with special
dressings that add the just-right flavor. When you think of
mealtime vegetables, why not think of salads? They're a wonderful
change-of-pace way to insure your family the vitamins and
minerals only vegetables can provide.

FOUR-BEAN SALADS

Spicy Herb Dressing (below)
1 can (16 ounces) cut green beans, drained
1 can (15½ ounces) wax beans, drained
1 can (15½ ounces) kidney beans, drained
1 can (15 ounces) garbanzo beans, drained
½ cup finely chopped green pepper
½ cup sliced pitted ripe olives
¼ cup sliced green onions
¼ cup snipped parsley
1 jar (2 ounces) sliced pimiento, drained and finely chopped
6 lettuce cups

Prepare Spicy Herb Dressing. Place remaining ingredients except lettuce cups in large bowl; toss with dressing. Cover and refrigerate at least 4 hours.

Drain salad, reserving dressing; spoon into lettuce cups. (Dressing can be refrigerated and used again within 1 week.)

6 servings.

Spicy Herb Dressing
½ cup sugar
½ cup wine vinegar
½ cup vegetable oil
1½ teaspoons salt
½ teaspoon dry mustard
½ teaspoon pepper
½ teaspoon red pepper sauce
¼ teaspoon dried basil leaves
¼ teaspoon garlic powder

Shake all ingredients in tightly covered jar.
About 1½ cups dressing.

BEAN SALADS, MEXICAN STYLE

1 can (16 ounces) whole green beans, drained
1 can (12 ounces) Mexican-style corn, drained
2 tablespoons finely chopped onion
½ cup bottled red French salad dressing
Dash of chili powder
½ cup shredded taco-seasoned or jalapeño pepper cheese (about 2 ounces)
6 lettuce cups
½ small onion, thinly sliced and separated into rings
Tortilla chips

Toss beans, corn and chopped onion with salad dressing. Cover and refrigerate at least 1 hour.

Sprinkle salad with chili powder; stir in cheese. Spoon salad into lettuce cups. Garnish with onion rings and serve with tortilla chips.

6 servings.

LEMON-LIMA SALADS

1 package (10 ounces) frozen green
   lima beans, cooked, drained and
   chilled
1 medium apple, coarsely chopped
2 tablespoons frozen lemonade
   concentrate, thawed
2 teaspoons vegetable oil
1 teaspoon prepared horseradish
4 lettuce cups
   Pomegranate seeds (optional)

Mix beans, apple, lemonade concentrate,
oil and horseradish. Spoon salad into lettuce
cups; sprinkle with pomegranate seeds.

4 servings.

FRUITED COLESLAW FOR A CROWD

1 medium head green cabbage
   (about 1½ pounds), coarsely
   shredded
4 medium carrots, grated
1 cup golden raisins
1 can (15½ ounces) crushed pineapple,
   drained (reserve 1 tablespoon syrup)
3 cups miniature marshmallows
¾ cup mayonnaise or salad dressing
3 tablespoons lemon juice
½ teaspoon salt

Reserve ½ cup of the cabbage, ¼ cup of
the carrots and 1 tablespoon of the raisins.
Mix remaining cabbage, carrots and raisins,
the pineapple, reserved pineapple syrup,
marshmallows, mayonnaise, lemon juice and
salt. Cover and refrigerate at least 1 hour.

To serve, arrange reserved cabbage, carrots
and raisins in shape of large flower in center of coleslaw.

12 servings.

ORANGE-CABBAGE SLAW

1 can (8 ounces) crushed pineapple in
   juice, drained
½ cup dairy sour cream
½ cup orange marmalade
2 tablespoons vinegar
¾ teaspoon salt
6 cups finely shredded green cabbage
   (about 1½ pounds)

Mix pineapple, sour cream, marmalade,
vinegar and salt; toss with cabbage. Cover
and refrigerate at least 2 hours.

10 servings.

RED CABBAGE SALAD

½ small head red cabbage, finely
   shredded or chopped
⅔ cup applesauce
½ cup golden raisins or chopped
   apple
2 to 3 teaspoons prepared horseradish
¼ teaspoon salt

Mix all ingredients. Cover and refrigerate
at least 1 hour.

4 servings.

CORNY COLESLAW
Pictured on page 37.

4 cups finely shredded green cabbage
   (about 1 pound)
1 jar (about 9 ounces) corn relish
⅓ cup sliced green onions
¼ teaspoon salt

Mix all ingredients. Cover and refrigerate at
least 1 hour.

4 servings.

VEGETABLE SALADS   43

CREAMY COLESLAW

Creamy Dressing (below)
6 cups finely shredded green cabbage
  (about 1½ pounds)
⅓ cup chopped onion
⅓ cup chopped cucumber

Prepare Creamy Dressing; toss with remaining ingredients.

6 servings.

Creamy Dressing
⅔ cup mayonnaise or salad dressing
2 tablespoons sugar
2 tablespoons vinegar
1 tablespoon milk
½ teaspoon salt
⅛ teaspoon paprika

Mix all ingredients; refrigerate at least 1 hour. *About 1 cup dressing.*

CUCUMBER SALAD

1 medium cucumber
½ cup vinegar
½ cup water
2 tablespoons sugar
¼ teaspoon salt
1 small onion, thinly sliced
  Salad greens

Run tines of fork lengthwise down side of unpared cucumber; cut into thin slices. Mix vinegar, water, sugar and salt; pour on cucumber and onion. Cover and refrigerate at least 2 hours. Just before serving, drain and serve on salad greens.

4 to 6 servings.

EGGPLANT SALAD

1 medium eggplant
¼ cup snipped parsley
3 tablespoons snipped chives
½ teaspoon salt
  Dash of pepper
1 tablespoon lemon juice
1 cup shredded Cheddar cheese
  (about 4 ounces)
¼ cup mayonnaise or salad dressing
  Parsley
  Thin tomato wedges

Cut a large lengthwise slice from 1 side of eggplant. Cut thin layer from opposite side to prevent tipping if necessary. Scoop out eggplant, leaving ½-inch wall. Cut eggplant into ½-inch pieces. Cover and refrigerate eggplant shell.

Cook and stir eggplant pieces, snipped parsley, chives, salt and pepper until eggplant is crisp-tender, about 5 minutes. Stir in lemon juice. Refrigerate until chilled, about 1½ hours.

Stir cheese and mayonnaise into eggplant mixture; spoon into eggplant shell. Serve salad on bed of parsley and garnish with tomato wedges.

4 servings.

LETTUCE WEDGES WITH CREAMY TOPPING

1 medium head iceberg lettuce
1 package (3 ounces) cream cheese, softened
½ cup dairy sour cream
1 small carrot, grated
2 tablespoons finely chopped green pepper
2 tablespoons shredded Cheddar cheese
1 teaspoon lemon juice
½ teaspoon salt
¼ teaspoon onion salt
    Paprika

Cut lettuce into 6 wedges. Place a lettuce wedge on each of 6 salad plates. Make 3 or 4 vertical cuts almost to bottom of each wedge. Mix remaining ingredients except paprika; spoon onto wedges. Sprinkle with paprika.

6 servings.

BROILED SALADS

1 large head iceberg lettuce
⅓ cup bottled French salad dressing
3 tablespoons mayonnaise or salad dressing
6 tablespoons grated Parmesan cheese
4 slices bacon, crisply fried and crumbled

Set oven control to broil and/or 550°. Cut lettuce into 6 wedges; place on ungreased baking sheet. Mix salad dressing and mayonnaise; brush onto surfaces of lettuce wedges. Sprinkle with cheese. Broil with tops 2 to 3 inches from heat just until dressing and cheese bubble, about 2½ minutes. Sprinkle with bacon.

6 servings.

MUSHROOMS ITALIAN

½ cup olive or vegetable oil
2 tablespoons vinegar
2 tablespoons lemon juice
1 teaspoon salt
½ teaspoon dried basil leaves
¼ teaspoon dry mustard
⅛ teaspoon pepper
1 clove garlic, crushed (optional)
8 ounces mushrooms, sliced
    Snipped parsley

Shake all ingredients except mushrooms and parsley in tightly covered jar; pour on mushrooms. Cover and refrigerate no longer than 2 hours. Drain mushrooms and sprinkle with snipped parsley.

4 servings.

DILLED CHEESE AND PEA SALADS

1 package (10 ounces) frozen green peas
1 cup diced mild Cheddar cheese (about 4 ounces)
2 large stalks celery, chopped
¼ cup chopped dill pickle
½ cup mayonnaise or salad dressing
½ teaspoon dried dill weed or 1½ teaspoons snipped fresh dill weed
¼ teaspoon salt
8 lettuce cups

Rinse frozen peas under running cold water to separate; drain. Toss peas, cheese, celery, pickle, mayonnaise, dill weed and salt. Spoon salad into lettuce cups.

8 servings.

TOMATO-MUSHROOM SALADS

   Oil-Lemon Dressing (below)
4 small tomatoes, cut into wedges
4 ounces mushrooms, thinly sliced
½ cup pitted ripe olives
¼ cup snipped parsley
4 or 5 Bibb or Boston lettuce cups

Prepare Oil-Lemon Dressing; toss with tomatoes, mushrooms, olives and parsley. Cover and refrigerate until chilled. Spoon salad into lettuce cups.

4 or 5 servings.

Oil-Lemon Dressing
¼ cup vegetable oil
2 tablespoons lemon juice
¼ teaspoon salt
   Dash of pepper

Shake all ingredients in tightly covered jar.
About ⅓ cup dressing.

TOMATO-CAULIFLOWER SALAD

⅓ cup bottled Italian salad dressing
¼ teaspoon salt
   Dash of pepper
4 small tomatoes, cut into wedges
2 cups cauliflowerets, cut into
   ¼- to ½-inch pieces
2 cups bite-size pieces curly endive
½ cup pimiento-stuffed olives
2 tablespoons snipped parsley
   Lettuce leaves

Mix salad dressing, salt and pepper; toss with tomatoes, cauliflower, endive, olives and parsley. Serve salad on lettuce.

6 to 8 servings.

PICNIC TOMATOES
Pictured on page 37.

3 hard-cooked eggs
1 tablespoon plus 1½ teaspoons
   mayonnaise, salad dressing or
   vinegar
¼ teaspoon dry mustard
⅛ teaspoon salt
⅛ teaspoon pepper
6 medium tomatoes
   Salt
   Pepper
6 parsley sprigs

Cut eggs lengthwise into halves. Slip out yolks; mash with fork. Stir in mayonnaise, mustard, ⅛ teaspoon salt and ⅛ teaspoon pepper. Fill egg whites with egg yolk mixture, heaping it up lightly.

Core tomatoes. Cut thin slice from stem end of each tomato; reserve slices. Remove pulp and juice from tomatoes; reserve for future use. Drain tomatoes cut sides down on paper towels 5 minutes. Sprinkle insides with salt and pepper. Press deviled egg half, yolk side up, into each tomato; top with tomato slice. Place parsley sprig on each tomato slice. Wrap tomatoes in plastic wrap; refrigerate at least 1 hour.

6 servings.

BULGUR AND TOMATO SALAD

2 cups boiling water
1 cup bulgur wheat
2 cups cherry tomatoes, cut into halves
3 tablespoons lemon juice
2 tablespoons snipped fresh mint leaves or 1 teaspoon dried mint leaves
2 tablespoons snipped chives
2 tablespoons snipped parsley
1 teaspoon salt
¼ teaspoon lemon pepper
Cherry tomatoes
Parsley

Pour water on bulgur; let stand 15 minutes. Drain. Mix bulgur, 2 cups tomatoes, the lemon juice, mint leaves, chives, 2 tablespoons parsley, the salt and lemon pepper. Cover and refrigerate 2 hours. Garnish with tomatoes and parsley.

6 to 8 servings.

EIGHT-VEGETABLE MARINADE

Pictured on page 37.

1 jar (about 7 ounces) marinated artichoke hearts
1⅓ cups bottled Italian salad dressing
¼ cup snipped parsley
1 package (10 ounces) frozen baby Brussels sprouts, thawed and drained
2 carrots, cut diagonally into slices
1 green pepper, cut into strips
1 cup cauliflower pieces
1 cup broccoli pieces
5 ounces mushrooms, cut into halves
1 medium cucumber, cut into ½-inch pieces

Mix artichoke hearts (with liquid), salad dressing and parsley. Toss remaining ingredients in large bowl; pour artichoke hearts and marinade on vegetables. Toss to coat all vegetables. Cover and refrigerate at least 2 hours.

Drain salad, reserving marinade. (Marinade can be refrigerated and used again within 1 week.)

10 servings.

VEGETABLES VINAIGRETTE

  Vinaigrette Dressing (below)
1 can (8 ounces) cut green beans,
  drained
1 can (8 ounces) stewed tomatoes,
  drained
1 can (4 ounces) button mushrooms,
  drained
1 small onion, thinly sliced and
  separated into rings
5 lettuce cups

Prepare Vinaigrette Dressing; toss with beans, tomatoes, mushrooms and onion. Cover and refrigerate at least 8 hours. Spoon salad into lettuce cups.

5 servings.

Vinaigrette Dressing
¼ cup vegetable oil
2 tablespoons vinegar
1 teaspoon celery salt
1 teaspoon dry mustard
½ teaspoon salt
1 clove garlic, finely chopped

Shake all ingredients in tightly covered jar.
About ⅓ cup dressing.

MACARONI-BEET SALAD

1 cup uncooked macaroni
1 cup chopped cooked beets
½ cup chopped sweet gherkin pickle
¼ cup chopped onion
3 tablespoons bottled French salad
  dressing
½ teaspoon salt
  Romaine leaves
  Dairy sour cream

Cook macaroni as directed on package; drain. Rinse with cold water. Mix macaroni,

beets, pickle and onion. Toss with salad dressing and salt. Cover and refrigerate at least 2 hours.

Line salad bowl with romaine leaves. Spoon salad into bowl and garnish with dollops of sour cream.

4 servings.

POTATO-BROCCOLI SALAD
Pictured on page 37.

1 package (10 ounces) frozen
  chopped broccoli
½ teaspoon salt
½ cup boiling water
1 cup cubed hot cooked potatoes
½ cup bottled oil-and-vinegar salad
  dressing
2 medium stalks celery, cut
  diagonally into slices
2 hard-cooked eggs, cut into fourths
⅓ medium head iceberg lettuce, torn
  into bite-size pieces
¾ teaspoon seasoned salt
¼ teaspoon lemon pepper

Sprinkle frozen broccoli with ½ teaspoon salt. Pour boiling water on broccoli in large bowl. Cover and let stand 3 minutes; drain. Stir in potatoes. Pour salad dressing on broccoli and potatoes. Cover and refrigerate at least 2 hours. Add remaining ingredients; toss.

8 servings.

NO-FUSS POTATO SALAD

1¾ cups boiling water
1 package (6 ounces) hash brown potatoes with onions
3 or 4 large stalks celery, chopped
¼ medium green pepper, finely chopped
1 jar (2 ounces) sliced pimiento, drained
1 cup shredded Cheddar cheese (about 4 ounces)
½ cup mayonnaise or salad dressing
1 teaspoon salt
½ teaspoon dry mustard
1 hard-cooked egg, sliced
2 tablespoons snipped parsley

Pour boiling water on potatoes. Let stand, stirring occasionally, until water is absorbed, about 30 minutes.

Stir celery, green pepper, pimiento, cheese, mayonnaise, salt and mustard into potatoes. Cover and refrigerate at least 1 hour. Garnish with egg slices and parsley.

6 to 8 servings.

POTATO SALAD

2 pounds potatoes (about 6 medium)
¼ cup finely chopped onion
¼ cup bottled Italian salad dressing
1 teaspoon salt
⅛ teaspoon pepper
½ cup mayonnaise or salad dressing
½ cup chopped celery
2 hard-cooked eggs, cut up

Heat 1 inch salted water (½ teaspoon salt to 1 cup water) to boiling. Add potatoes. Heat to boiling; reduce heat. Cover and cook until tender, 30 to 35 minutes. Drain

potatoes; cool. Cut potatoes into cubes; stir in onion, salad dressing, salt and pepper. Cover and refrigerate at least 2 hours.

Just before serving, toss with mayonnaise until potatoes are well coated. Stir in celery and eggs.

4 to 6 servings.

HOT GERMAN POTATO SALAD

3 pounds potatoes (about 9 medium)
6 slices bacon
¾ cup chopped onion
2 tablespoons flour
2 tablespoons sugar
2 teaspoons salt
½ teaspoon celery seed
   Dash of pepper
¾ cup water
⅓ cup vinegar

Heat 1 inch salted water (½ teaspoon salt to 1 cup water) to boiling. Add potatoes. Heat to boiling; reduce heat. Cover and cook until tender, 30 to 35 minutes. Drain potatoes; cool.

Fry bacon in 10-inch skillet until crisp; remove from skillet and drain on paper towels. Cook and stir onion in bacon fat until tender and golden brown. Stir in flour, sugar, salt, celery seed and pepper. Cook over low heat, stirring constantly, until bubbly. Remove from heat; stir in water and vinegar. Heat to boiling, stirring constantly. Boil and stir 1 minute.

Crumble bacon. Cut potatoes into thin slices. Stir bacon and potatoes gently into hot mixture. Heat, stirring gently, until potatoes are coated and mixture is hot.

5 or 6 servings.

CUCUMBER SALAD MOLD

1 cup boiling water
1 package (3 ounces) lime-flavored gelatin
1 cup dairy sour cream
1 cup unsweetened pineapple juice
1 package (3 ounces) lime-flavored gelatin
½ cup lemon juice
1 teaspoon salt
4 medium cucumbers, shredded and drained (about 2 cups)°
  Salad greens
  Cucumber slices

Pour boiling water on 1 package gelatin in bowl; stir until gelatin is dissolved. Beat in sour cream with hand beater until smooth. Pour into 6-cup mold. Refrigerate just until set, about 2 hours.

Heat pineapple juice to boiling. Pour boiling pineapple juice on 1 package gelatin in bowl; stir until gelatin is dissolved. Stir in lemon juice and salt. Refrigerate until very thick, about 1½ hours.

Stir shredded cucumbers into gelatin mixture in bowl; pour on gelatin mixture in mold. Refrigerate until firm, at least 4 hours. Unmold on salad greens and garnish with cucumber slices.

10 to 12 servings.

°Cucumbers can be finely chopped in food grinder and drained.

AVOCADO MOLDED CROWN

Pictured on page 38.

2 envelopes unflavored gelatin
1 cup cold water
1 can (13¾ ounces) chicken broth
½ cup bottled green goddess salad dressing
¼ cup mayonnaise or salad dressing
2 medium avocados, cut up
¼ cup lemon juice
½ cup mayonnaise or salad dressing
1 small onion
¼ teaspoon salt
¼ teaspoon pepper
⅛ teaspoon red pepper sauce
9 drops green food color
3 drops yellow food color
  Lemon slices
  Watercress

Sprinkle gelatin on cold water in saucepan to soften; stir over low heat until gelatin is dissolved. Remove from heat. Stir in broth. Measure ½ cup of the gelatin mixture; reserve remaining gelatin mixture. Beat green goddess dressing and ¼ cup mayonnaise into the ½ cup gelatin mixture; pour into 6-cup mold. Refrigerate just until set, about 40 minutes.

Place avocado pieces in blender container; pour lemon juice on avocado pieces. Add reserved gelatin mixture, ½ cup mayonnaise, the onion, salt, pepper, pepper sauce and food colors. Cover and blend until smooth, about 10 seconds. Refrigerate until slightly thickened, about 30 minutes.

Pour avocado mixture gently on gelatin in mold. Refrigerate until firm, at least 6 hours. Unmold salad on serving plate and garnish with lemon slices and watercress.

8 servings.

VEGETABLE RING

4 envelopes unflavored gelatin
1 can (10½ ounces) condensed beef broth
1 can (46 ounces) cocktail vegetable juice
1 can (16 ounces) mixed vegetables, drained
4 large stalks celery, coarsely chopped
1 medium zucchini, chopped (about 1 cup)
1 tablespoon lemon juice
¼ teaspoon salt
4 drops red pepper sauce
  Yogurt Dressing (below)
  Parsley

Sprinkle gelatin on broth in 3-quart saucepan to soften; stir over low heat until gelatin is dissolved, about 3 minutes. Remove from heat; stir in vegetable juice, mixed vegetables, celery, zucchini, lemon juice, salt and pepper sauce. Pour into 12-cup ring mold. Refrigerate until firm, at least 8 hours. (Some vegetables may sink to the bottom; some may rise to the top. Stir when slightly thickened to distribute vegetables evenly.)

Prepare Yogurt Dressing. Unmold salad on serving plate. Garnish with parsley and serve with dressing.

12 to 16 servings.

Yogurt Dressing
1 carton (8 ounces) unflavored yogurt
¼ cup mayonnaise or salad dressing
¼ teaspoon salt
  Paprika

Mix yogurt, mayonnaise and salt; sprinkle with paprika. *About 1 cup dressing.*

INDIVIDUAL TOMATO ASPICS

1 envelope unflavored gelatin
2 cups tomato juice
1 tablespoon lemon juice
2 teaspoons vinegar
½ teaspoon salt
⅛ teaspoon onion juice
3 drops red pepper sauce
½ cup chopped celery
¼ cup chopped cucumber
  Bibb lettuce
  Mayonnaise or salad dressing

Sprinkle gelatin on ½ cup of the tomato juice in saucepan to soften; stir over low heat until gelatin is dissolved. Stir into remaining tomato juice; stir in lemon juice, vinegar, salt, onion juice and pepper sauce. Refrigerate until slightly thickened, about 25 minutes.

Stir celery and cucumber into gelatin mixture; pour into individual molds. Refrigerate until firm, at least 3 hours. Unmold on lettuce and serve with mayonnaise.

4 servings.

CONFETTI SOUFFLE

Pictured on page 38.

2 envelopes unflavored gelatin
¾ cup cold water
⅔ cup mayonnaise or salad dressing
2 tablespoons vinegar
1 tablespoon prepared mustard
¼ teaspoon salt
⅛ teaspoon pepper
1 cup cut-up green cabbage
1 medium carrot, cut into 1-inch pieces
⅓ medium cucumber, cut into 1-inch pieces
½ small onion, cut into halves
6 radishes, cut into halves
1 jar (2 ounces) diced pimiento, drained
3 egg whites
¼ teaspoon cream of tartar
  Cucumber slices
  Radish slices
  Mayonnaise or salad dressing

Make a 4-inch-wide band of triple thickness aluminum foil 2 inches longer than circumference of 4-cup soufflé dish. Extend depth of dish by securing foil band around top of dish.

Sprinkle gelatin on cold water in 2-quart saucepan to soften; stir over low heat until gelatin is dissolved. Remove from heat; stir in ⅔ cup mayonnaise, the vinegar, mustard, salt and pepper. Refrigerate until mixture mounds slightly when dropped from a spoon, 20 to 30 minutes.

Place cabbage, carrot, cucumber pieces, onion and radish halves in blender container; pour enough water on vegetables to cover. Cover and blend on medium to high speed until vegetables are chopped,

7 or 8 seconds. Drain thoroughly. Fold chopped vegetables and pimiento into gelatin mixture.

Beat egg whites and cream of tartar in small mixer bowl until stiff but not dry. Fold gelatin mixture into egg whites in large bowl. Turn mixture into soufflé dish. Refrigerate until firm, at least 4 hours. Remove band and garnish with cucumber and radish slices; serve with mayonnaise.

6 servings.

JELLIED BORSCH

1 can (16 ounces) shoestring beets, drained (reserve liquid)
2 envelopes unflavored gelatin
1½ teaspoons instant beef bouillon
2 cups finely shredded green or red cabbage
2 tablespoons snipped chives
1 tablespoon lemon juice
½ teaspoon salt
½ cup dairy sour cream
1 tablespoon snipped parsley
  Leaf lettuce

Add enough water to reserved beet liquid to measure 2 cups. Sprinkle gelatin on liquid in 1½-quart saucepan to soften; stir in instant bouillon. Stir over low heat until gelatin and bouillon are dissolved. Remove from heat; cool 5 minutes. Stir in beets, cabbage, chives, lemon juice and salt. Pour into baking pan, 8x8x2 or 9x9x2 inches. Refrigerate until mixture mounds slightly when dropped from a spoon, about 30 minutes.

Mix sour cream and parsley; swirl through beet mixture. Refrigerate until firm, at least 2 hours. Serve on lettuce.

8 or 9 servings.

MAIN-DISH SALADS

Satisfying Combinations That Make Almost a Meal

Here come the big taste-budding ones! Salads bringing protein-rich, hunger-stopping meat, poultry, fish and eggs blissfully together with delicious counterpoint basics. Virtually brimming with vim and vigor, these salads are ready to carry the meal. And to complete the feast, you'll find a tasty array of salad-enhancing breads. All that's needed is a beverage. Brunch, lunch and supper need never be quite the same again . . . with all hands happier and better off for it!

CHEF'S SMORGASBORD SALAD
Pictured on the cover.

Clear French Dressing (below)
3 cups bite-size pieces leaf lettuce
3 cups bite-size pieces spinach
3 cups bite-size pieces iceberg lettuce
3 cups bite-size pieces red leaf lettuce
8 slices bacon, crisply fried and crumbled
1 jar (about 7 ounces) marinated artichoke hearts, drained
1 cup croutons
2 hard-cooked eggs, chopped
2 to 3 cups ¼-inch strips fully cooked ham or turkey (8 to 12 ounces)
1 cup shredded Cheddar cheese (about 4 ounces)
½ cup chopped peanuts or cashews
½ cup sliced pitted ripe olives
½ cup sliced cucumbers
¼ cup sliced green onions
2 to 3 tablespoons chopped anchovies

Prepare Clear French Dressing. Arrange leaf lettuce, spinach, iceberg lettuce and red leaf lettuce in separate sections in large salad bowl. Place remaining ingredients in small containers around salad bowl. Serve with dressing.

6 to 8 servings.

Clear French Dressing
¾ cup olive oil, vegetable oil or combination
⅓ cup wine or tarragon vinegar
2¼ teaspoons salt
2 or 3 cloves garlic, crushed
¾ teaspoon monosodium glutamate
⅛ teaspoon pepper

Shake all ingredients in tightly covered jar. *About 1 cup dressing.*

HAM, RED BEAN AND RICE SALAD

1⅓ cups water
⅔ cup uncooked regular rice
½ teaspoon salt
1 bay leaf
Snappy Dressing (below)
1 can (15½ ounces) red kidney beans, chilled and drained°
3 tablespoons finely chopped onion
½ large stalk celery, chopped
¼ teaspoon garlic salt
½ medium green pepper, chopped
2 cups ½-inch cubes fully cooked ham, chilled
Celery leaves

Heat water, rice, salt and bay leaf to boiling, stirring once or twice; reduce heat. Cover and simmer 14 minutes. (Do not lift cover or stir.) Remove from heat; fluff lightly with fork. Cover and let steam 5 to 10 minutes. Refrigerate until chilled.

Prepare Snappy Dressing. Mix beans, onion, celery and garlic salt. Mix rice and green pepper. Arrange bean mixture, rice mixture and ham cubes in separate sections on platter. Garnish with celery leaves and serve with dressing.

5 servings.

°1½ cups cooked black beans can be substituted for the kidney beans.

Snappy Dressing
½ cup mayonnaise or salad dressing
¼ cup catsup
¼ teaspoon ground cumin
¼ teaspoon aromatic bitters

Mix all ingredients. *¾ cup dressing.*

Salade Niçoise (page 68) — a stylishly simple choice. Perfect for a luncheon or light supper.

Salads to serve as the main course. Clockwise from top left: Salad Lovers' Lasagne (page 58), Triple Decker Club Salad (page 63), Oriental Chicken Salad (page 66), Crab-Shrimp-Avocado Salad (page 67).

HAM-SESAME SEED SALAD

Oil-and-Vinegar Dressing (below)
2 cups cubed fully cooked ham
½ medium head iceberg lettuce, torn into bite-size pieces
½ medium cucumber, thinly sliced
2 green onions, thinly sliced lengthwise and cut into 1½-inch pieces
1 medium tomato, cut into thin wedges
2 tablespoons toasted sesame seed (see note)
Monterey Jack cheese, cut into ¼-inch strips (optional)

Prepare Oil-and-Vinegar Dressing. Toss with ham, lettuce, cucumber, onions, tomato and sesame seed. Garnish with cheese.

6 to 8 servings.

Note: To toast sesame seed, heat oven to 350°. Bake in ungreased baking pan, stirring occasionally, until golden, 8 to 10 minutes.

Oil-and-Vinegar Dressing
1 tablespoon vegetable oil
1 tablespoon vinegar
1½ teaspoons sugar
¾ teaspoon salt
½ teaspoon monosodium glutamate
1 small clove garlic, crushed

Shake all ingredients in tightly covered jar.
About ⅛ cup dressing.

HAM SALADS HAWAIIAN

Potato Nests (below)
1½ cups finely chopped fully cooked ham
⅓ cup mayonnaise or salad dressing
1 can (13¼ ounces) pineapple chunks, drained
1 large stalk celery, chopped
2 teaspoons finely chopped onion
¼ teaspoon prepared mustard
Dash of garlic powder (optional)

Prepare Potato Nests. Mix remaining ingredients; refrigerate at least 1 hour. Fill Potato Nests with salad.

5 servings.

Potato Nests
Heat oven to 400°. Empty 1 package (6 ounces) hash brown potatoes with onions into bowl. Pour enough very hot water on potatoes to cover; let stand 10 minutes. Drain completely. Toss potatoes with 1 egg, beaten, and 1 teaspoon salt. Press about ¼ cup potato mixture firmly and evenly against bottom and side of each of 10 greased 6-ounce custard cups. Place on baking sheet. Bake until edges are brown and crisp, 35 to 40 minutes. Remove from cups, loosening edges with knife if necessary. Cool on wire rack.

LENTIL-HAM SALAD

6 cups water
1 cup lentils
2 cups chopped fully cooked ham
½ cup bottled oil-and-vinegar salad
　dressing with herbs
¼ cup sliced green onions
¼ cup sliced pitted ripe olives
1 teaspoon salt
½ teaspoon pepper
　Lettuce leaves
　Parsley

Heat water and lentils to boiling; reduce heat. Cover and simmer 3 minutes; remove from heat. Let stand 1 to 2 hours.

Drain lentils; stir in ham, salad dressing, onions, olives, salt and pepper. Cover and refrigerate at least 1 hour.

Line salad bowl with lettuce leaves. Spoon salad into bowl and garnish with parsley.

4 servings.

PICNIC ROLL-UPS

6 slices salami or boiled ham
6 large lettuce leaves
　Mayonnaise or salad dressing
6 thin slices mozzarella cheese
　Lettuce leaves
　Tomato wedges

Place 1 salami slice on each of 6 lettuce leaves; spread mayonnaise over salami. Top each salami slice with cheese slice; roll up lettuce leaves. Cut roll-ups into bite-size pieces; secure with wooden picks. Serve roll-ups on lettuce. Garnish with tomato wedges.

6 servings.

SALAD LOVERS' LASAGNE
Pictured on page 56.

　Lasagne Dressing (below)
1 package (7 ounces) macaroni shells
1 cup shredded pizza cheese (about
　4 ounces)
4 medium zucchini, chopped
½ cup sliced pitted ripe olives
　Salad greens
1 can (8 ounces) tomato sauce
　(optional)
8 slices salami
　Grated Parmesan cheese

Prepare Lasagne Dressing. Cook macaroni as directed on package; drain. Rinse with cold water. Toss macaroni, pizza cheese, zucchini and olives with dressing. Cover and refrigerate at least 3 hours.

Place salad greens on 8 salad plates. Spoon salad onto greens; drizzle each salad with about 2 tablespoons tomato sauce. Cut each salami slice into a spiral, about ¼ inch wide; arrange 1 slice on each salad. Serve with Parmesan cheese.

8 servings.

Lasagne Dressing
1 can (8 ounces) tomato sauce
½ cup mayonnaise or salad dressing
1 teaspoon salt
½ teaspoon garlic salt
½ teaspoon dried oregano leaves

Place all ingredients in blender container. Cover and blend on medium speed until smooth, about 10 seconds. *1½ cups dressing.*

SALAD-SIDE BREADS

Spreads, shakings and special touches that help to make all sorts of breads sensational salad partners.

French Mustard Slices

1 package (10 ounces) brown-and-serve French bread
¼ cup butter or margarine, softened
2 tablespoons snipped parsley
1 tablespoon prepared mustard
1 teaspoon instant minced onion
1 teaspoon lemon juice

Heat oven to 400°. Cut loaf diagonally into 1-inch slices. Mix remaining ingredients; spread on slices. Reassemble loaf; place on ungreased baking sheet. Bake about 15 minutes. *About 24 slices.*

Hickory French Bread

1 loaf (1 pound) French bread
½ cup butter or margarine, softened
1 cup shredded natural sharp Cheddar cheese (about 4 ounces)
1 tablespoon snipped parsley
½ teaspoon hickory-smoked salt
2 teaspoons Worcestershire sauce

Cut loaf diagonally into 1-inch slices. Mix remaining ingredients; spread on slices. Reassemble loaf; wrap in piece of heavy-duty aluminum foil, 28 × 18 inches, and seal securely. Heat in 350° oven 20 minutes. *About 24 slices.*

Hot Chili French Bread: Omit parsley and hickory-smoked salt. Decrease Worcestershire sauce to 1 teaspoon and mix in 1 to 2 teaspoons chopped hot chili peppers.

Spicy English Muffins

½ cup butter or margarine, softened
1 teaspoon chili powder
½ teaspoon onion salt
4 English muffins, split into halves

Set oven control to broil and/or 550°. Mix butter, chili powder and onion salt; spread on cut surfaces of muffin halves. Broil with tops about 3 inches from heat until golden brown, 2 to 3 minutes. *4 servings.*

Hot Bread in Foil

Cut 1 loaf (1 pound) French bread into 1-inch slices or cut Vienna, rye or pumpernickel bread into ½-inch slices. Spread generously with ½ cup butter or margarine, softened, or with 1 of the Butter Spreads (below). Reassemble loaf; wrap in piece of heavy-duty aluminum foil, about 28 × 18 inches, and seal securely. Heat in 400° oven 15 to 20 minutes. *About 24 slices.*

Butter Spreads: Mix ½ cup butter or margarine, softened, with 1 of the following:
☐ *Garlic*—1 medium clove garlic, finely chopped, or ⅛ teaspoon garlic powder
☐ *Onion*—2 tablespoons finely chopped onion or snipped chives
☐ *Seeded*—1 to 2 teaspoons celery, poppy, dill or sesame seed
☐ *Tarragon*—1 teaspoon dried tarragon leaves and ¼ teaspoon paprika

BRAUNSCHWEIGER LOAF

½ cup tomato juice
¼ cup cold water
1 envelope unflavored gelatin
¾ pound Braunschweiger
1 cup tomato juice
¾ cup finely chopped celery
½ cup mayonnaise or salad dressing
¼ cup chopped green pepper
¼ cup chopped pimiento-stuffed
   olives
¼ cup finely chopped green onions
2 tablespoons lemon juice
2 teaspoons sugar
½ teaspoon salt
½ teaspoon dry mustard
⅛ teaspoon pepper
⅛ teaspoon ground cloves
   Salad greens
1 package (10 ounces) frozen asparagus
   spears, cooked, drained and chilled
1 tomato, sliced
2 hard-cooked eggs, sliced

Mix ½ cup tomato juice and the water. Sprinkle gelatin on juice mixture in 2-quart saucepan to soften; stir over low heat until gelatin is dissolved. Refrigerate until slightly thickened.

Soften Braunschweiger by mashing with spoon. Stir Braunschweiger, 1 cup tomato juice, the celery, mayonnaise, green pepper, olives, onions, lemon juice, sugar, salt, mustard, pepper and cloves into gelatin mixture. Pour into loaf pan, 9x5x3 inches. Refrigerate until firm. Unmold on salad greens; arrange asparagus and tomato and egg slices around loaf.

6 to 8 servings.

MARINATED BEEF AND MUSHROOMS

1½-pound beef sirloin steak,
   1½ inches thick
1 jar (4½ ounces) sliced mushrooms,
   drained
1 medium green pepper, sliced into
   thin rings
⅓ cup red wine vinegar
¼ cup vegetable oil
1 teaspoon salt
½ teaspoon onion salt
½ teaspoon Worcestershire sauce
¼ teaspoon pepper
¼ teaspoon dried tarragon leaves,
   crushed
2 cloves garlic, crushed
4 lettuce cups
   Cherry tomatoes

Set oven control to broil and/or 550°. Broil steak with top 2 inches from heat until medium, about 13 minutes on each side. Cool; cut into ⅜-inch strips. Arrange strips in ungreased baking dish, 13½x8¾x1¾ inches. Place mushrooms on steak; top with green pepper rings. Mix vinegar, oil, salt, onion salt, Worcestershire sauce, pepper, tarragon and garlic; pour on steak and vegetables. Cover and refrigerate at least 3 hours, spooning vinegar mixture over vegetables occasionally.

Remove vegetables to lettuce cups with slotted spoon. Place steak next to vegetables and garnish with tomatoes.

4 servings.

TOSTADA SALADS

Guacamole Dressing (below)
1 pound ground beef
¾ cup water
1 package (1¼ ounces) taco
   seasoning mix
1 can (15½ ounces) red kidney beans,
   drained
¾ teaspoon salt
¼ teaspoon chili powder
6 tostadas
   Six ½-inch slices iceberg lettuce
½ cup shredded taco-seasoned or
   jalapeño pepper cheese (about 2
   ounces)
3 tomatoes, cut into thin wedges

Prepare Guacamole Dressing. Cook and stir ground beef in 10-inch skillet over medium-high heat until brown; drain. Stir in water, seasoning mix, beans, salt and chili powder. Heat to boiling; reduce heat. Cover and simmer 10 minutes.

Place 1 tostada on each of 6 salad plates; top with lettuce slice. Cut each lettuce slice about ¼ inch deep in crisscross pattern. Spoon ½ cup beef mixture onto each lettuce slice; sprinkle with cheese. Garnish with tomato wedges and serve with dressing.

6 servings.

Guacamole Dressing
1 avocado
1 small onion, finely chopped
2 canned green chili peppers, seeded
   and chopped (about 2 teaspoons)
1½ teaspoons lemon juice
½ teaspoon salt
¼ teaspoon pepper
   Mayonnaise or salad dressing

Mash avocado; beat in onion, chili peppers, lemon juice, salt and pepper until creamy. Spoon dressing into dish. Spread with thin layer of mayonnaise to prevent discoloration. Cover and refrigerate. Stir gently just before serving. *About ¾ cup dressing.*

LIVER-TOMATO-ONION SALADS

1 cup biscuit baking mix
½ teaspoon salt
1 pound beef liver, cut into
   4x¾-inch strips
½ cup buttermilk
2 tablespoons shortening
   Lettuce leaves
2 medium tomatoes, thinly sliced
½ to 1 medium Bermuda onion,
   thinly sliced
¼ cup imitation bacon
   Bottled Thousand Island or
   blue cheese salad dressing

Mix baking mix and salt; dip liver strips into baking mix, then into buttermilk and again into baking mix. Heat shortening in 10-inch skillet over medium heat until melted. Cook liver strips in shortening until brown, about 5 minutes on each side.

Place lettuce leaves on 4 salad plates. Arrange tomato and onion slices alternately down centers of leaves; sprinkle with imitation bacon. Arrange liver strips around tomato and onion slices. Serve salads with salad dressing.

4 servings.

GOURMET PLATTER

1 package (6½ ounces) wild-and-white rice mix
1 cup shredded Swiss cheese (about 4 ounces)
½ cup mayonnaise or salad dressing
¼ cup half-and-half
1 teaspoon dry mustard
½ teaspoon salt
¼ to ½ teaspoon dried rosemary leaves
12 strips Swiss cheese, 3x½x½ inch
12 thin slices smoked tongue
   Leaf lettuce
   Cherry tomatoes
   Parsley

Cook rice as directed on package; cool slightly. Stir in 1 cup cheese, the mayonnaise, half-and-half, mustard, salt and rosemary. Cover and refrigerate at least 2 hours.

Place 1 cheese strip on each tongue slice; roll up. Arrange rice mixture and tongue rolls on lettuce. Garnish with tomatoes and parsley.

6 servings.

CHILLED VEAL AND FRUIT SALAD

2 cups cut-up cooked veal
1 cup halved seeded Tokay grapes
1 medium green pepper, cut into strips
1 tablespoon lemon juice
½ teaspoon salt
2 bananas
2 tablespoons mayonnaise or salad dressing
2 tablespoons instant nonfat dry milk
1 tablespoon water
   Leaf lettuce
¼ cup toasted chopped pecans

Mix veal, grapes, green pepper, lemon juice and salt. Cover and refrigerate at least 2 hours.

Mash half of 1 banana; stir in mayonnaise, dry milk and water. Slice remaining bananas; add to veal mixture. Toss with banana-mayonnaise mixture. Serve on lettuce; sprinkle with pecans.

6 servings.

CRUNCHY DEVILED EGG SALADS

5 hard-cooked eggs, coarsely chopped
1 large stalk celery, chopped
1 tablespoon chopped onion
1 cup shoestring potatoes
⅓ cup mayonnaise or salad dressing
¾ teaspoon dry mustard
½ teaspoon salt
  Dash of ground marjoram (optional)
4 lettuce cups
  Parsley
1 hard-cooked egg, sliced

Toss chopped eggs, celery, onion, potatoes, mayonnaise, mustard, salt and marjoram. Spoon salad into lettuce cups. Garnish with parsley and egg slices.

4 servings.

CHOW MEIN CHICKEN SALADS

3 cups cut-up cooked chicken, chilled
1 cup chopped watermelon pickles
2 tablespoons chopped onion
2 large stalks celery, coarsely chopped
¾ cup mayonnaise or salad dressing
1 teaspoon salt
½ teaspoon curry powder
  Dash of pepper
1 cup chow mein noodles
6 lettuce cups
  Chow mein noodles

Mix chicken, pickles, onion, celery, mayonnaise, salt, curry powder and pepper. Stir in 1 cup chow mein noodles. Spoon salad into lettuce cups and garnish with chow mein noodles.

6 servings.

TRIPLE DECKER CLUB SALADS

Pictured on page 56.

  Thousand Island Dressing (below)
2 heads Bibb or Boston lettuce, torn
  into bite-size pieces
4 medium tomatoes or 2 beefsteak
  tomatoes, peeled and sliced
2 cups ¼-inch strips cooked chicken
  or turkey (about 8 ounces), chilled
4 slices bacon, cut into 1-inch
  pieces and crisply fried

Prepare Thousand Island Dressing. Divide lettuce among 4 individual salad plates; top with tomatoes, chicken and bacon. Serve with dressing.

4 servings.

Thousand Island Dressing
½ cup mayonnaise or salad dressing
1 hard-cooked egg, chopped
1 tablespoon chili sauce
1 tablespoon chopped pimiento-stuffed
  olives
¼ teaspoon paprika
  Dash of salt
  Dash of pepper

Mix all ingredients. Cover and refrigerate at least 24 hours. *About ¾ cup dressing.*

"YOUR BRAND" SALAD DRESSINGS

"Personal caring"—it's the only ingredient the production line can't handle. Here are a few old-time basic dressings to try when you'd rather do it yourself.

Mayonnaise
1 egg yolk
1 teaspoon dry mustard
1 teaspoon sugar
¼ teaspoon salt
 Dash of cayenne red pepper
2 tablespoons lemon juice
1 cup vegetable oil

Beat egg yolk, mustard, sugar, salt, red pepper and 1 tablespoon lemon juice in small mixer bowl on medium speed until blended. Beat in vegetable oil, 1 drop at a time; increase rate of addition as mixture thickens. Beat in remaining lemon juice; refrigerate. *About 1 cup dressing.*

Russian Dressing: Mix ½ cup Mayonnaise, ¼ cup chili sauce and a few drops onion juice. *About ¾ cup dressing.*

Red French Dressing
1 cup vegetable oil
⅔ cup catsup
½ cup vinegar
½ cup sugar
2 tablespoons minced onion
1 tablespoon lemon juice
1 teaspoon salt
1 teaspoon pepper
1 teaspoon dry mustard
1 teaspoon paprika

Shake all ingredients in tightly covered jar. Refrigerate at least 3 hours. *2⅔ cups dressing.*

Cooked Salad Dressing
¼ cup all-purpose flour
2 tablespoons sugar
1 teaspoon salt
1 teaspoon dry mustard
1½ cups milk
2 egg yolks, slightly beaten
⅓ cup vinegar
1 tablespoon butter or margarine

Mix flour, sugar, salt and mustard in 2-quart saucepan. Stir milk gradually into egg yolks; slowly stir into flour mixture. Heat to boiling over medium heat, stirring constantly. Boil and stir 1 minute. Remove from heat; stir in vinegar and butter. Cool slightly; refrigerate. *About 2 cups dressing.*

Italian Salad Dressing
1 cup vegetable oil
¼ cup lemon juice
¼ cup white vinegar
1 teaspoon salt
1 teaspoon sugar
½ teaspoon dried oregano leaves
½ teaspoon dry mustard
½ teaspoon onion salt
½ teaspoon paprika
⅛ teaspoon ground thyme
2 cloves garlic, crushed

Shake all ingredients in tightly covered jar. Refrigerate at least 2 hours. *1½ cups dressing.*

DOUBLE-LAYER CHICKEN MOLD

    2 hard-cooked eggs, sliced
      Pimiento-stuffed olive halves
    4 cups cut-up cooked chicken (see note)
    2 cups chicken broth
    3 tablespoons water
    1 tablespoon lemon juice
    ¾ teaspoon salt
 1½ envelopes unflavored gelatin
      (1 tablespoon plus 1½ teaspoons)
    ¾ cup chopped pimiento-stuffed
      olives
    1 cup boiling water
    1 package (3 ounces) lemon-flavored
      gelatin
    ½ cup cold water
    ½ cup mayonnaise or salad dressing
    3 tablespoons vinegar or lemon juice
    ¼ teaspoon salt
    2 large stalks celery, finely chopped
    ¼ cup snipped parsley
    1 tablespoon plus 1½ teaspoons
      finely chopped onion
      Salad greens

Arrange egg slices and olive halves alternately in 8-cup ring mold; cover with 2 cups of the chicken. Mix broth, 3 tablespoons water, the lemon juice and ¾ teaspoon salt in saucepan. Sprinkle unflavored gelatin on broth mixture to soften; stir over low heat until gelatin is dissolved. Remove from heat; cool slightly. Stir in chopped olives. Pour broth mixture on chicken. Refrigerate until mixture mounds slightly when dropped from a spoon, about 2 hours.

Pour boiling water on flavored gelatin in bowl; stir until gelatin is dissolved. Stir in ½ cup water, the mayonnaise, vinegar and ¼ teaspoon salt; pour into ice cube tray. Freeze until firm around edges but soft in center, 15 to 20 minutes. Pour into bowl; beat with hand beater until fluffy. Stir in remaining chicken, the celery, parsley and onion; pour on mixture in mold. Refrigerate until firm, at least 4 hours. Unmold on salad greens.

12 servings.

Note: A 3- to 4-pound broiler-fryer chicken yields 3 to 4 cups cut-up cooked chicken.

CHICKEN-SPINACH SALAD WITH BACON

      Piquant Dressing (below)
    2 cups cut-up cooked chicken or turkey
    5 ounces spinach, torn into bite-size
      pieces
    2 cups broccoli flowerets, cut into
      ¼-inch pieces
    1 can (8½ ounces) water chestnuts,
      drained and sliced
    4 slices bacon, crisply fried and
      crumbled
      Grated Parmesan cheese (optional)

Prepare Piquant Dressing; pour on chicken. Cover and refrigerate at least 15 minutes. Toss chicken with spinach, broccoli and water chestnuts; sprinkle with bacon. Serve with cheese.

6 servings.

Piquant Dressing
    2 tablespoons soy sauce
    1 tablespoon vinegar
    1 tablespoon vegetable oil
    ½ teaspoon instant minced onion
    ¼ teaspoon sugar
    ⅛ teaspoon pepper

Shake all ingredients in tightly covered jar. *¼ cup dressing.*

ORIENTAL CHICKEN SALAD

Pictured on page 56.

2 ounces uncooked maifun (rice stick) noodles*
  Ginger Dressing (below)
½ bunch romaine, torn into bite-size pieces
2 cups cut-up cooked chicken or turkey, chilled
¼ cup sliced green onions

Prepare noodles as directed on package for crispy noodles; drain. Prepare Ginger Dressing; toss with noodles and the remaining ingredients.

6 servings.

*6 cups chow mein noodles can be substituted for the maifun noodles; toss with Ginger Dressing and remaining ingredients.

Ginger Dressing

¼ cup vegetable oil
3 tablespoons vinegar
2 teaspoons sugar
1 teaspoon soy sauce
¾ teaspoon salt
½ teaspoon pepper
½ teaspoon monosodium glutamate
¼ teaspoon ground ginger

Shake all ingredients in tightly covered jar.
½ cup dressing.

HOT CHICKEN SALAD IN AVOCADO SHELLS

1 can (about 7 ounces) marinated artichoke hearts, drained and sliced
1 can (5 ounces) boned chicken, drained (about ½ cup)
1 jar (2 ounces) sliced pimiento, drained
⅓ cup mayonnaise or salad dressing
½ large stalk celery, chopped
½ teaspoon salt
½ teaspoon chili powder
3 avocados
½ cup shredded taco-seasoned or jalapeño pepper cheese (about 2 ounces)

Heat oven to 400°. Mix artichoke hearts, chicken, pimiento, mayonnaise, celery, salt and chili powder. Cut each avocado lengthwise into halves; remove pit. Cut thin layer from bottom of each half to prevent tipping if necessary. Place avocado halves cut sides up in ungreased baking pan, 9x9x2 inches. Spoon about ¼ cup chicken mixture onto each half, spreading to cover entire cut surface; sprinkle with cheese. Bake uncovered until chicken mixture is hot and cheese is melted, about 20 minutes.

6 servings.

CRAB-SHRIMP-AVOCADO SALAD

Pictured on page 56.

Creamy Dill Dressing (below)
1 can (8½ ounces) water chestnuts, drained and sliced
1 package (6 ounces) frozen crabmeat, thawed, drained and cartilage removed
2 cans (4½ ounces each) large shrimp, drained
1 medium cucumber, chopped
¼ cup sliced green onions
2 avocados, sliced
2 medium tomatoes, cut into wedges
Lettuce leaves or cups

Prepare Creamy Dill Dressing; toss with water chestnuts, crabmeat, shrimp, cucumber and onions. Cover and refrigerate at least 1 hour.

Arrange avocados and tomatoes on lettuce. Top with crabmeat mixture.

4 or 5 servings.

Creamy Dill Dressing

½ cup mayonnaise or salad dressing
¼ cup dairy sour cream
2 tablespoons lemon juice
¼ teaspoon salt
¼ teaspoon dried dill weed

Mix all ingredients. *About ¾ cup dressing.*

MEDITERRANEAN SALADS

1 cup cauliflowerets, cut into 1-inch pieces
1 small onion, sliced and separated into rings
½ medium green pepper, coarsely chopped
1 medium carrot, thinly sliced
1 stalk celery, coarsely chopped
½ cup dry red or white wine
¼ cup tarragon vinegar
1 small clove garlic, crushed
1 bay leaf
1 can (8 ounces) tomato sauce
1 can (6½ ounces) tuna, drained
1 can (4 ounces) mushroom stems and pieces, drained
8 small pimiento-stuffed olives
6 romaine leaves
6 anchovy fillets
6 celery leaves

Mix cauliflowerets, onion, green pepper, carrot, celery, wine, vinegar, garlic and bay leaf in 3-quart saucepan. Heat to boiling; reduce heat. Cover and simmer 3 minutes; stir in tomato sauce. Heat to boiling; reduce heat. Cover and simmer 3 minutes longer. Remove from heat; stir in tuna, mushrooms and olives. Cover and refrigerate at least 2 hours.

Spoon about 1 cup wine mixture onto each romaine leaf with slotted spoon. Garnish each salad with rolled-up anchovy fillet and celery leaf.

6 servings.

SALADE NIÇOISE

Pictured on page 55.

1 package (10 ounces) frozen
   French-style green beans
   French Dressing (below)
2 heads Bibb or Boston lettuce,
   torn into bite-size pieces
2 tomatoes, cut into sixths
2 hard-cooked eggs, cut into
   fourths
1 can (about 7 ounces) tuna, drained
2 tablespoons sliced pitted ripe
   olives, drained
6 anchovies
   Snipped parsley

Cook beans as directed on package; drain. Refrigerate until chilled. Prepare French Dressing. Place lettuce in salad bowl. Arrange beans, tomatoes and eggs around edge of salad. Mound tuna in center; sprinkle with olives. Garnish with anchovies and sprinkle with parsley; serve with dressing.

4 servings.

French Dressing
½ cup olive oil, vegetable oil or
   combination
2 tablespoons vinegar
2 tablespoons lemon juice
½ teaspoon salt
¼ teaspoon dry mustard
¼ teaspoon paprika

Shake all ingredients in tightly covered jar.
¾ cup dressing.

TUNA ON A SHOESTRING

1 can (6½ ounces) tuna, drained
1 cup shredded carrots
1 cup chopped celery
¼ cup finely chopped onion
¾ to 1 cup mayonnaise or salad
   dressing
1 can (4 ounces) shoestring potatoes
   Carrot curls (optional)

Toss tuna, carrots, celery, onion and mayonnaise until tuna is well coated with mayonnaise. Cover and refrigerate at least 1 hour.

Just before serving, fold in potatoes. Garnish with carrot curls.

4 to 6 servings.

TUNA-BEAN TOSS

1 can (16 ounces) cut green beans,
   drained
1 can (15 ounces) garbanzo beans,
   drained
1 can (8 ounces) green lima beans,
   drained
1 can (9¼ ounces) tuna, drained
2 large stalks celery, chopped
¾ cup mayonnaise or salad dressing
¼ cup lemon juice
1 tablespoon instant minced onion
½ teaspoon lemon pepper
¼ teaspoon garlic salt
¼ teaspoon salt
2 hard-cooked eggs, sliced
3 tablespoons snipped parsley

Mix beans, tuna, celery, mayonnaise, lemon juice, onion, lemon pepper, garlic salt and salt. Cover and refrigerate at least 1 hour. Garnish with egg slices and parsley.

8 servings.

FAMILY FAVORITE TUNA SALADS

1 package (7 ounces) macaroni
  shells or rings
2 cans (6½ ounces each) tuna,
  drained
1 jar (4½ ounces) pimiento-stuffed
  olives, drained and cut into halves
5 large stalks celery, chopped
½ to ¾ cup mayonnaise or salad
  dressing
2 teaspoons lemon juice
1 teaspoon onion salt
½ teaspoon celery salt
½ teaspoon salt
9 lettuce cups
  Tomato wedges or sliced hard-cooked
  eggs
  Parsley sprigs

Cook macaroni as directed on package; drain. Rinse with cold water. Toss macaroni, tuna, olives, celery, mayonnaise, lemon juice, onion salt, celery salt and salt. Cover and refrigerate at least 1 hour. Spoon salad into lettuce cups and garnish with tomato wedges and parsley sprigs.

9 servings.

TUNA-CANTALOUPE SALADS

1 package (6 ounces) frozen
  Chinese pea pods
3 cups cooked rice
2 cans (6½ ounces each) tuna, drained
⅓ cup mayonnaise or salad dressing
1 teaspoon instant chicken bouillon
¼ teaspoon ground ginger
3 small cantaloupes
⅓ cup cashews or salted peanuts,
  coarsely chopped

Rinse frozen pea pods under running cold water to separate; drain. Mix pea pods, rice, tuna, mayonnaise, instant bouillon and ginger. Cover and refrigerate at least 2 hours.

Cut cantaloupes crosswise into halves, using zigzag or scalloped cut; scoop out seeds. Cut thin layer from bottom of each half to prevent tipping if necessary. Spoon 1 cup rice mixture into each half; sprinkle with cashews.

6 servings.

TUNA-BROCCOLI MOLD

  1 package (10 ounces) frozen chopped broccoli
 10 pimiento-stuffed olives, cut into halves
  2 cans (6½ ounces each) tuna, drained
  2 tablespoons finely chopped onion
  1 envelope unflavored gelatin
 1½ cups chicken broth
  3 tablespoons lemon juice
  ½ teaspoon salt
    Pale salad greens
    Mayonnaise or salad dressing

Cook broccoli as directed on package; drain. Arrange olive halves cut sides down in 4-cup mold; spread broccoli evenly over olive halves. Mix tuna and onion; press evenly over broccoli.

Sprinkle gelatin on broth in saucepan to soften; stir over low heat until gelatin is dissolved. Remove from heat; stir in lemon juice and salt. Pour gelatin mixture carefully on tuna mixture. Refrigerate until firm. Unmold on salad greens and serve with mayonnaise.

4 or 5 servings.

VARIATIONS

Chicken-Broccoli Mold: Substitute 2 cans (5 ounces each) boned chicken, drained, for the tuna and omit salt.

Salmon-Broccoli Mold: Substitute 1 can (16 ounces) red salmon, drained and flaked, for the tuna.

FESTIVE TUNA MOLD

  1 can (10¾ ounces) condensed chicken broth
  ½ cup water
  1 envelope unflavored gelatin
  2 cans (9¼ ounces each) tuna, drained
  2 jars (2 ounces each) diced pimiento, drained
  6 hard-cooked eggs, chopped
  4 large stalks celery, finely chopped
  1 medium avocado, sliced
  2 teaspoons grated lemon peel
  2 teaspoons salt
  ¼ teaspoon pepper
  1 cup chilled whipping cream
    Salad greens

Mix broth and water in 3-quart saucepan. Sprinkle gelatin on broth mixture to soften; stir over low heat until gelatin is dissolved. Refrigerate until slightly thickened, about 50 minutes.

Stir tuna, pimiento, eggs, celery, avocado, lemon peel, salt and pepper into gelatin mixture. Beat cream in chilled small mixer bowl until stiff; fold into tuna mixture. Pour into baking pan, 9x9x2 inches. Refrigerate until firm, at least 4 hours. Serve on salad greens.

8 servings.

INDEX

Antipasto toss, 20
Apple(s)
  -cheese wedges, 22
  Waldorf salads, 22
Apricot
  orange-, salad, 39
  salad, frosted, 34
  salad, moonglow, 22
Asparagus and watercress toss, 10
Avocado(s), 28
  crab-shrimp-, salad, 67
  molded crown, 50
  shells, hot chicken salad in, 66
  spinach-, salad, 13

Banana-spinach toss, 15
Bananas, 28
Bean(s)
  four-bean salads, 42
  lemon-lima salads, 43
  salads, Mexican style, 42
  tuna-, toss, 68
Bean sprouts, tossed goddess, 10
Beef
  and mushrooms, marinated, 60
  tostada salads, 61
Beet(s)
  jellied borsch, 52
  macaroni-, salad, 48
  pineapple-, salads, pink, 26
Berry
  cherry-, salads, 31
  -wine salad, 31
Black cherry mold, 39
Blueberry-pineapple squares, 40
Borsch, jellied, 52
Braunschweiger loaf, 60
Breads, salad-side, 59
Broiled salads, 45
Brussels sprouts
  spinach and sprouts salad, 12
Bulgur and tomato salad, 47
Burmese rice-fruit salad, 25

Cabbage
  corny coleslaw, 43
  creamy coleslaw, 44
  fruited coleslaw for a crowd, 43
  orange-, slaw, 43
  red, salad, 43

Caesar salad, great, 7
Canned fruit salad plate, 29
Cantaloupe-tuna salads, 69
Cauliflower-tomato salad, 46
Cheese and pea salads, dilled, 45
Chef's smorgasbord salad, 54
Cherry
  -berry salads, 31
  -grape salads, 22
  -pineapple salad, 39
Chicken
  -broccoli mold, 70
  mold, double-layer, 65
  salad, hot, in avocado shells, 66
  salad, Oriental, 66
  salads, chow mein, 63
  -spinach salad with bacon, 65
  triple decker club salads, 63
Chilled veal and fruit salad, 62
Chow mein chicken salads, 63
Coleslaw
  corny, 43
  creamy, 44
  fruited, for a crowd, 43
  orange-cabbage slaw, 43
Color toss, 13
Confetti soufflé, 52
Corny coleslaw, 43
Crab-shrimp-avocado salad, 67
Creamy coleslaw, 44
Creamy lettuce toss, 7
Crunchy deviled egg salads, 63
Cucumber
  salad, 44
  salad mold, 50
Curried Waldorf salads, 22

Deviled egg salads, crunchy, 63
Dilled cheese and pea salads, 45
Double-layer chicken mold, 65

Eggplant salad, 44
Eight-vegetable marinade, 47
Endive-fruit salad, 15

Family favorite tuna salads, 69
Fantastic green salad, 8
Festive tuna mold, 70
Flaming spinach salad, 9
Four-bean salads, 42
Fresh fruit on crispy noodles, 30
Fresh peach and pear salads, 24
Frosted apricot salad, 34
Fruit
  bowl, summer, 30
  canned, salad plate, 29
  fresh, on crispy noodles, 30
  ring mold, pastel, 33
  salad, pineapple, 26

Fruit (continued)
  salad, starburst, 29
  salad, tropical, 29
  salad, winter, 27
  sunny citrus salad, 16
  24-hour salad, 27
Fruit salads, 21–40
Fruited coleslaw for a crowd, 43

Garbanzo and zucchini toss, 12
Glossy red, white and green
  salad, 20
Gourmet platter, 62
Gourmet tossed green salad, 8
Grape
  cherry-, salads, 22
  -pea salad, 19
Grapefruit-orange salads, 23
Great Caesar salad, 7
Green salads, 5–20
Greens, 11
Greens and tomato-tomato, 10

Ham
  chef's smorgasbord salad, 54
  lentil-, salad, 58
  picnic roll-ups, 58
  red bean and rice salad, 54
  salads Hawaiian, 57
  –sesame seed salad, 57
Hot chicken salad in avocado
  shells, 66
Hot German potato salad, 49
Hula salads, 25

Individual tomato aspics, 51

Jellied borsch, 52

Kiwi fruit, 28

Lemon-lima salads, 43
Lentil-ham salad, 58
Lettuce, 11
  broiled salads, 45
  toss, creamy, 7
  wedges with creamy topping,
    45
Liver-tomato-onion salads, 61

Macaroni
  -beet salad, 48
  family favorite tuna salads, 69
  -pineapple toss, 26
  salad lovers' lasagne, 58
Main dish salads, 53–70
Mandarin salad, 16
Mangoes, 28

Maple nut Waldorf salads, 22
Marinated beef and mushrooms, 60
Mediterranean salads, 67
Minted pineapple toss, 19
Mixed greens with garlic dressing, 9
Molasses waldorf salads, 22
Molded salads, 32
  avocado molded crown, 50
  berry-wine salad, 31
  black cherry mold, 39
  Braunschweiger loaf, 60
  cherry-berry salads, 31
  cherry-pineapple salad, 39
  chicken-broccoli mold, 70
  confetti soufflé, 52
  cucumber salad mold, 50
  double-layer chicken mold, 65
  festive tuna mold, 70
  frosted apricot salad, 34
  individual tomato aspics, 51
  jellied borsch, 52
  orange-apricot salad, 39
  orange-buttermilk salad, 40
  pastel fruit ring mold, 33
  pineapple-blueberry squares, 40
  raspberry-peach salads, 33
  salmon-broccoli mold, 70
  strawberry-rhubarb mold, 31
  tuna-broccoli mold, 70
  vegetable ring, 51
  watermelon mold, 34
Moonglow apricot salad, 22
Mushrooms Italian, 45

No-fuss potato salad, 49

Orange(s)
  -apricot salad, 39
  -buttermilk salad, 40
  -cabbage slaw, 43
  grapefruit-, salads, 23
  mandarin salad, 16
  -onion salads, 23
  shady glade salad, 24
  toss, 19
Oriental chicken salad, 66

Papayas, 28
Pastel fruit ring mold, 33
Peach
  and pear salads, fresh, 24
  raspberry-, salads, 33
  salads, 24
  salads with molasses cream, 25
Peanut butter Waldorf salads, 22
Pear and peach salads, fresh, 24

Peas
  color toss, 13
  dilled cheese and pea salads, 45
  grape-pea salad, 19
Pickle-cheese toss, 13
Picnic roll-ups, 58
Picnic tomatoes, 46
Pineapple(s), 28
  -beet salads, pink, 26
  -blueberry squares, 40
  Burmese rice-fruit salad, 25
  cherry-, salad, 39
  fruit salad, 26
  hula salads, 25
  macaroni-, toss, 26
  toss, minted, 19
Pink pineapple-beet salads, 26
Pomegranates, 28
Potato
  -broccoli salad, 48
  salad, 49
  salad, hot German, 49
  salad, no-fuss, 49

Raspberry-peach salads, 33
Red cabbage salad, 43
Rhubarb-strawberry mold, 31

Salad dressings, 14, 64
  blue cheese-lemon dressing, 16
  cheese dressing, 29
  classic French dressing, 8
  clear French dressing, 54
  cooked salad dressing, 64
  French dressing, 68
  green goddess dressing, 10
  Italian salad dressing, 64
  mayonnaise, 64
  no-oil dressing, 24
  old-fashioned fruit dressing, 27
  red French dressing, 64
  ruby blue cheese dressing, 23
  Russian dressing, 64
  thousand island dressing, 63
  vinegar-oil dressing, 12
Salad lovers' lasagne, 58
Salade Niçoise, 68
Salade Provençale, 7
Salami
  picnic roll-ups, 58
  salad lovers' lasagne, 58
Salmon-broccoli mold, 70
Shady glade salad, 24
Shrimp
  cocktail toss, 20
  -crab-avocado salad, 67
  glossy red, white and green salad, 20
Smorgasbord salad, chef's, 54

Spinach
  and sprouts salad, 12
  -avocado salad, 13
  banana-, toss, 15
  salad, flaming, 9
Starburst fruit salad, 29
Strawberry(-ies)
  berry-wine salad, 31
  cherry-berry salads, 31
  freeze, 33
  -rhubarb mold, 31
Summer fruit bowl, 30
Sunny citrus salad, 16

Tomato(es)
  aspics, individual, 51
  bulgur and, salad, 47
  -cauliflower salad, 46
  -mushroom salads, 46
  picnic, 46
Tongue
  gourmet platter, 62
Tossed goddess bean sprouts, 10
Tossed green salads, 5–20
Tostada salads, 61
Triple decker club salads, 63
Tropical fruit salad, 29
Tuna
  -bean toss, 68
  -broccoli mold, 70
  -cantaloupe salads, 69
  Mediterranean salads, 67
  mold, festive, 70
  on a shoestring, 68
  salade Niçoise, 68
  salads, family favorite, 69
Turkey
  chef's smorgasbord salad, 54
  Oriental chicken salad, 66
  triple decker club salads, 63
24-hour salad, 27

Veal and fruit salad, chilled, 62
Vegetable ring, 51
Vegetable salads, 41–52
Vegetables vinaigrette, 48

Waldorf salads, 22
  curried, 22
  maple nut, 22
  molasses, 22
  peanut butter, 22
Watercress and asparagus toss, 10
Watermelon mold, 34
Winter fruit salad, 27

Zucchini
  garbanzo and, toss, 12
  salad, 12